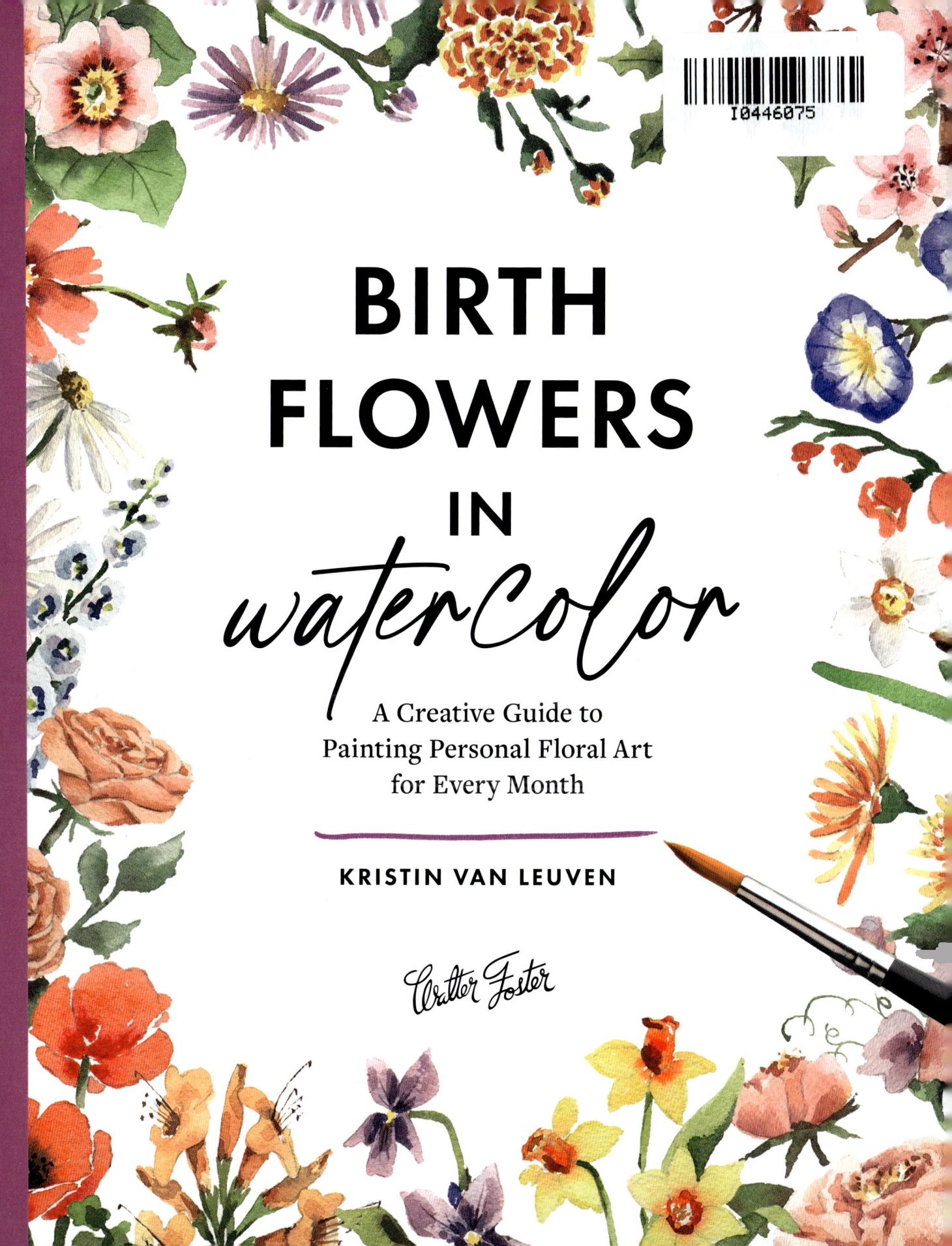

BIRTH FLOWERS
IN
watercolor

A Creative Guide to Painting Personal Floral Art for Every Month

KRISTIN VAN LEUVEN

Walter Foster

CONTENTS

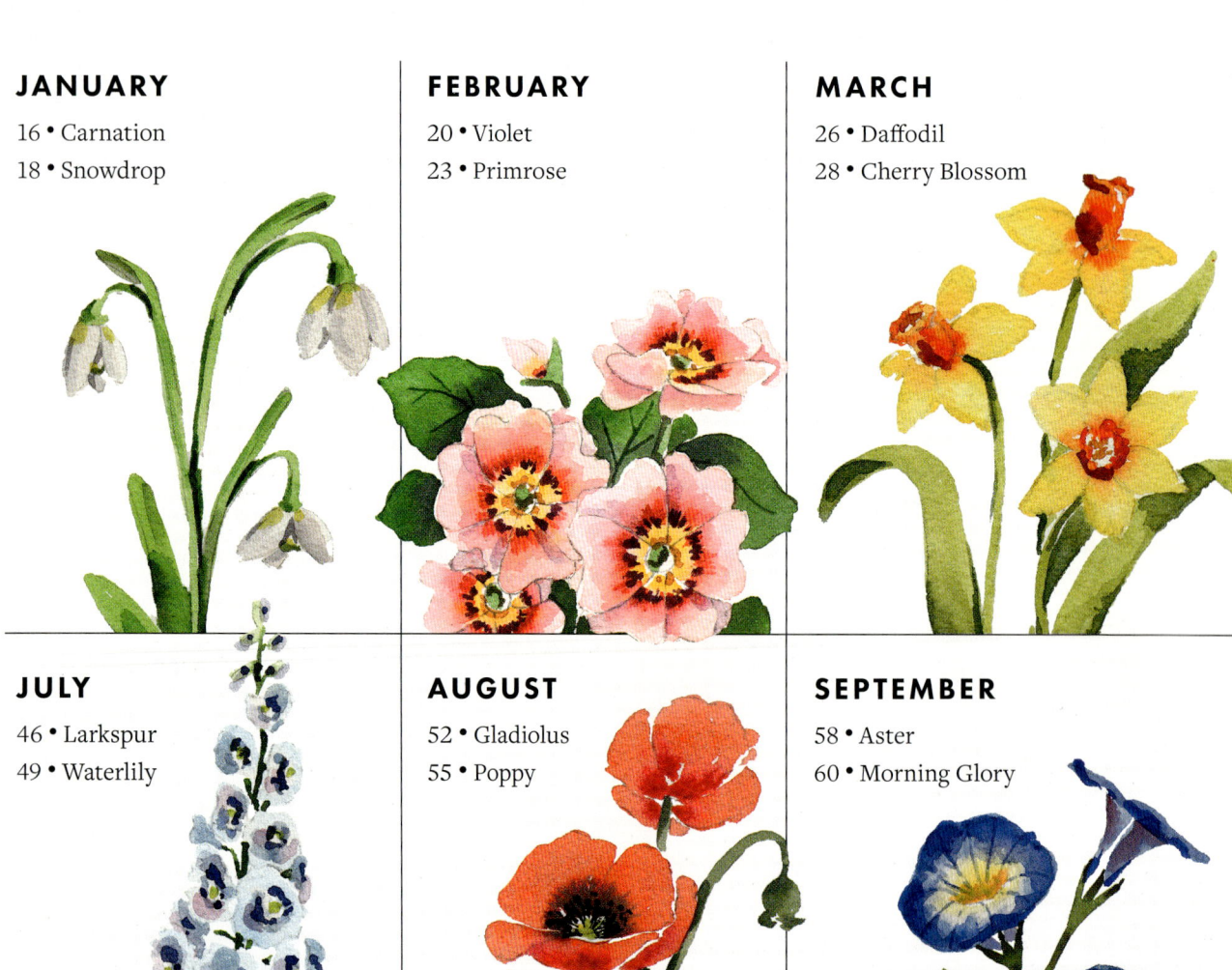

APRIL

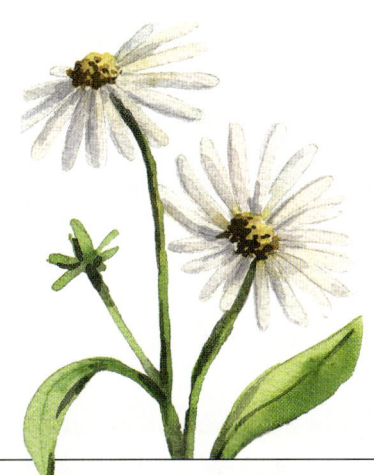

MAY

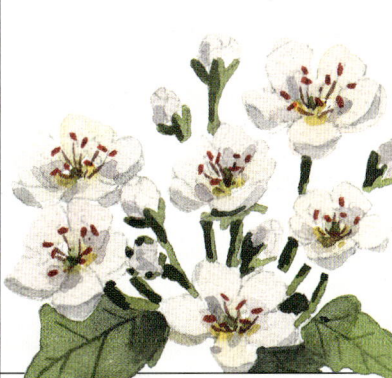

JUNE

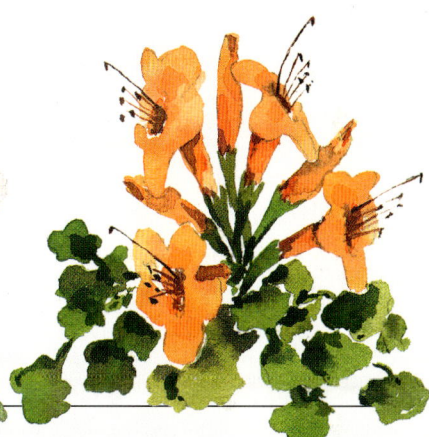

OCTOBER

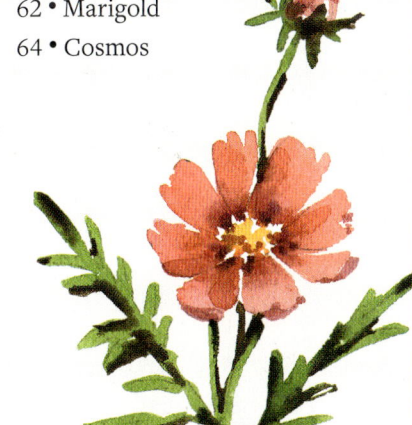

NOVEMBER

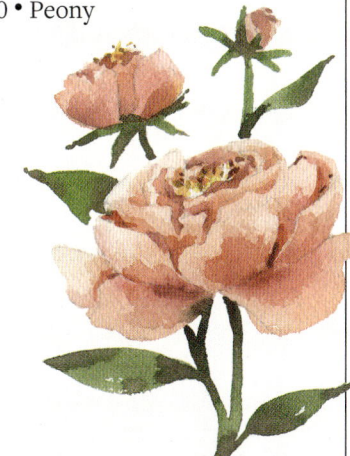

DECEMBER

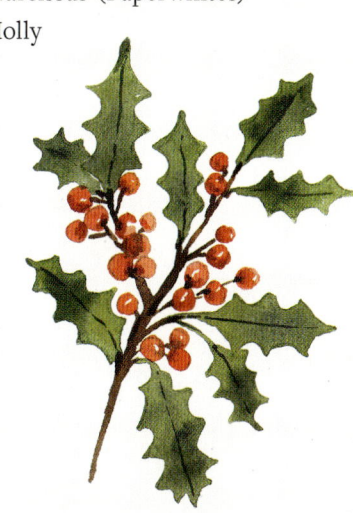

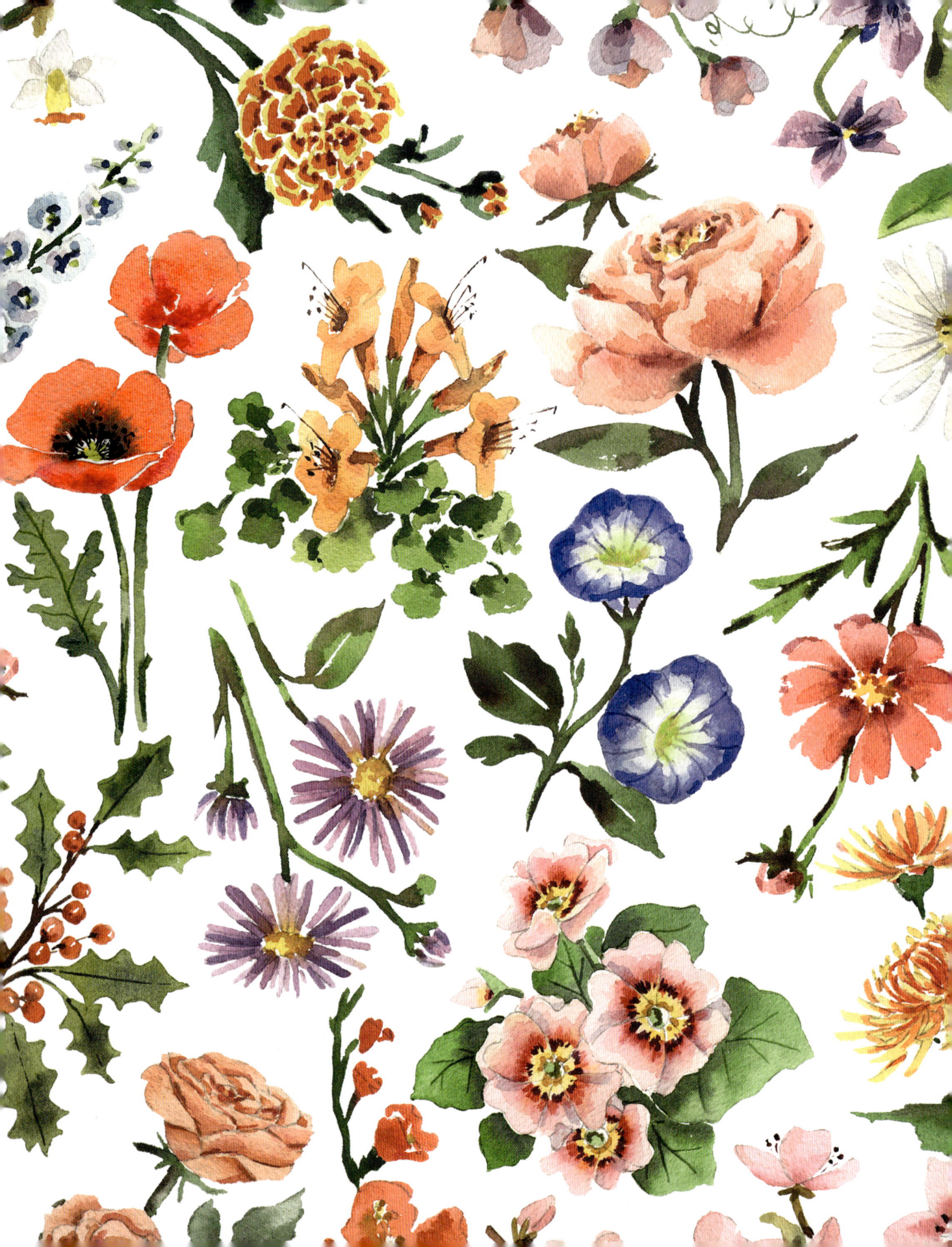

WHAT ARE BIRTH FLOWERS?

HELLO! I'm so glad you're here with me to paint the beautiful flowers in this book. You will learn and grow so much while also having fun with watercolor, and I can't wait to teach you all about the beautiful birth month flowers we're painting.

Birth month flowers have a long history, dating back to ancient times when flowers were believed to hold special meanings and powers. The tradition of associating flowers with specific months likely originated in Roman and Greek cultures, where each month was linked to a particular flower to honor deities or celebrate seasonal changes. Over time, these associations evolved into a way of representing personal traits, emotions, and characteristics tied to an individual's birth month. Each flower carries its own symbolism—such as love, strength, or purity—reflecting the qualities of those born during that month. For example, the January birth flower, carnation, symbolizes love and fascination, while the December birth flower, narcissus (a.k.a. paperwhites), represents good wishes, respect, and faithfulness. Today, these flowers continue to hold significance as a personal and cultural symbol, often used in celebrations like birthdays and floral arrangements.

In this book, we're going to be painting twenty-four flowers—the most common two associated with each month of the year. First, we'll talk about the materials you'll need, such as the brushes and paints. Then I'll show you watercolor techniques that bring flowers to life. Plus, I'll show you how to mix colors for an array of shades.

Each flower includes a QR code that gives you exclusive access to a video showing the step-by-step process of painting each flower. At the back of the book, you'll find a watercolor paper pad with each birth month flower sketched and ready to paint. So, all you need to do is paint along with the instructions and you'll be on your way to a lovely collection of floral paintings. If you're interested in tracing the outlines onto your own paper, scan the QR code on page 79 and you'll be able to download the sketch templates for each flower to print at home.

Let's get started!

MATERIALS AND SUPPLIES

Watercolor Paint

The two most popular forms of watercolor are tubes and pans, each with its own advantages and unique characteristics. Watercolor tubes allow you to create your own palette and choose the colors you want to work with. You can squeeze out as much paint as needed, making it ideal for large washes or when a vibrant, bold color is required. On the other hand, watercolor pans are small, solid cakes of pigment that require wetting with a brush to activate the color. The choice between tubes and pans comes down to personal preference and the specific needs of a project. For the birth flowers in this book, I use watercolor pans.

PAINT COLORS

I prefer to use a limited split-primary palette of cool colors and warm colors with two extras. The cool primaries are lemon yellow, permanent rose, and

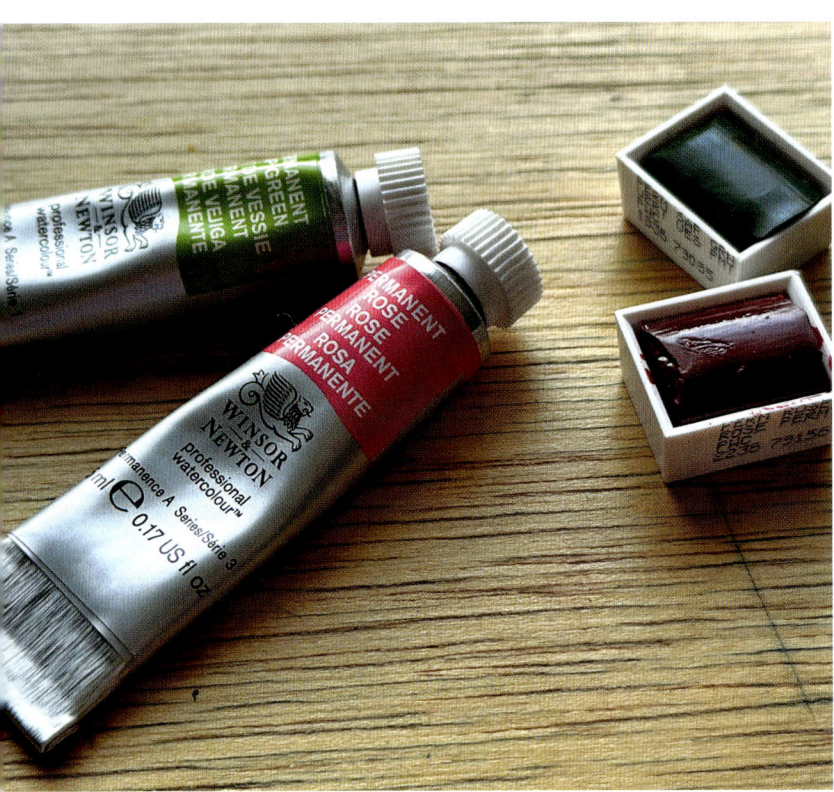

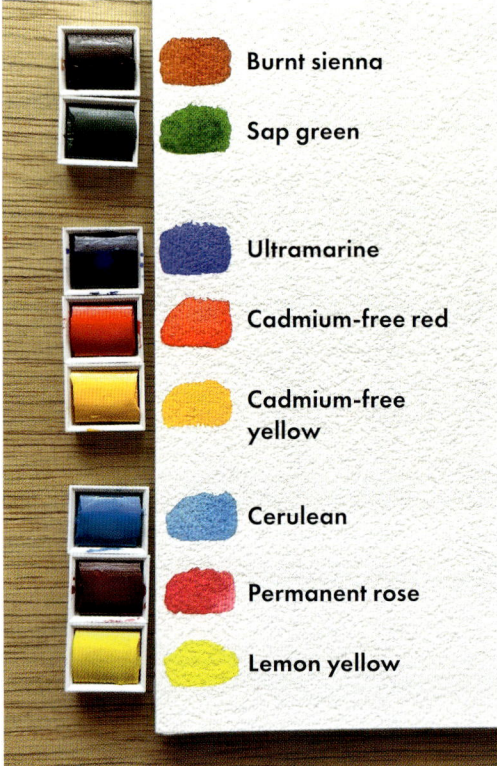

Burnt sienna

Sap green

Ultramarine

Cadmium-free red

Cadmium-free yellow

Cerulean

Permanent rose

Lemon yellow

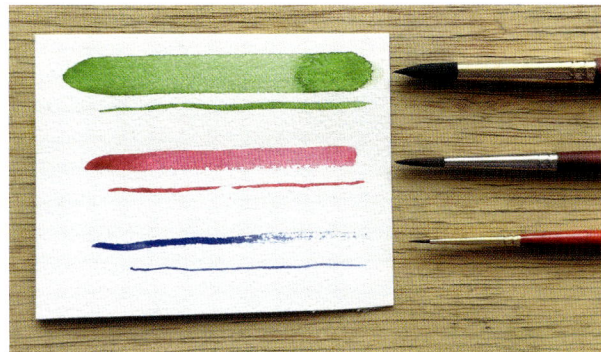

cerulean. The warm primaries are cadmium-free yellow, cadmium-free red, and ultramarine. I also added sap green and burnt sienna for a great green and brown readily available without mixing. Using these two sets of primaries, we can mix every single color you can imagine. We will go over color mixing soon, but feel free to use premixed colors if you prefer.

Watercolor Brushes

For these flower projects, we don't need any fancy brushes. One good round brush either a size 4 or 6 will work great. If you want to try different sizes of brushes for larger washes or smaller details, the ones I use are size 8 round, size 4 round, and size 3/0 round.

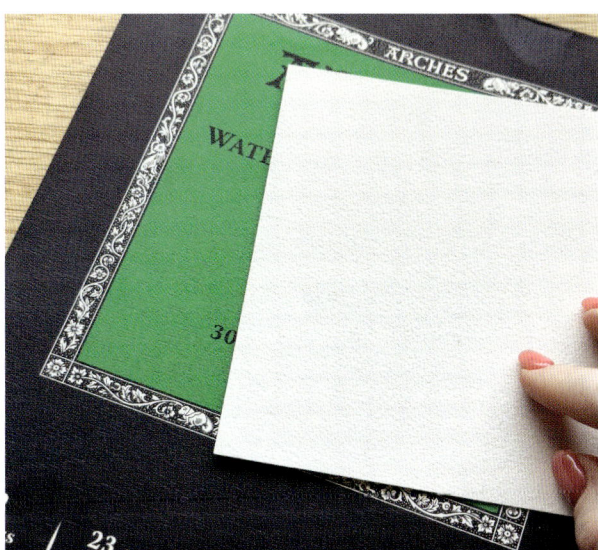

Watercolor Paper

There are many great options for watercolor paper, including smooth, hot-pressed, cold-pressed, and rough. My preference is 140 lb (300 gsm) cold-pressed cotton paper. It has just enough texture and absorption that the paints flow and do what you want, without being too smooth or rough. Everyone will have their own preference based on how they want their paintings to look. The paper provided with this book is a great paper to start with and practice your watercolor techniques. You can also use transfer paper to transfer over the flower outlines onto your paper of choice (see page 8) or use the QR code on page 79 to download the templates and print them on the paper of your choice.

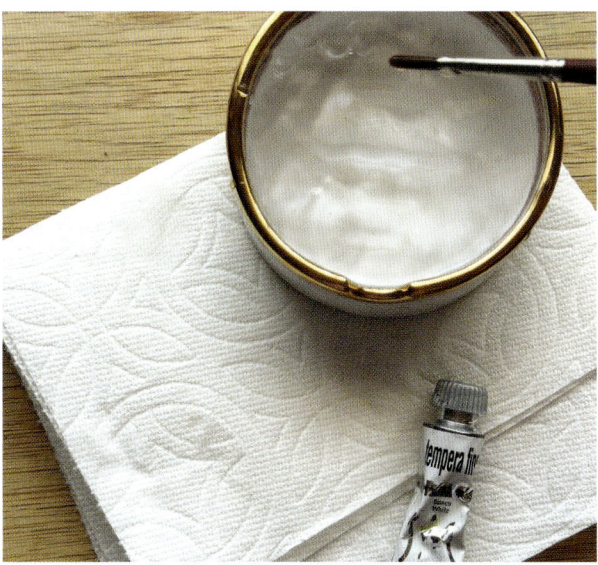

Other: Paper Towel, Water, and White Gouache

The only other materials you will need are water, paper towel or cloth, and occasionally white gouache for details. I try not to use white paint, but it can come in handy for a tiny highlight.

TRANSFERRING SKETCHES

The watercolor paper pad included with this book is a great place to practice your techniques and paint lovely samples. At some point, you may want to use other papers to achieve a different look. Or, perhaps, you have several family members born in a particular month, so you want to make more than one. Use the technique outlined here to transfer sketches to the paper of your choice.

1 To transfer the flower outlines onto your preferred paper, you will need tracing paper. Use the QR code provided on page 79 to download and print the flower sketches on basic copy paper. Print the outlines on printer paper at the right size for your watercolor paper and place your tracing paper on top.

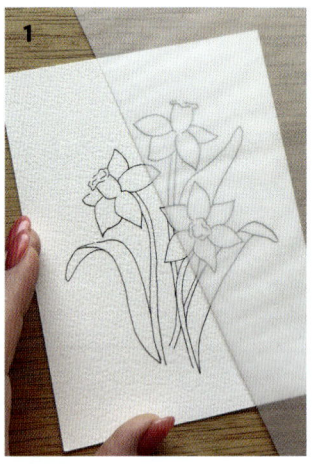

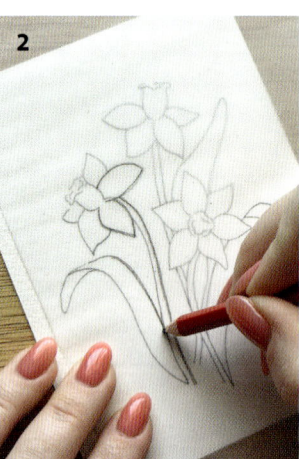

2 Follow the outline on the paper with a pencil until the entire outline is sketched onto the tracing paper. Then, if you don't want the image reversed, flip the tracing paper over and copy your lines on the opposite side of the tracing paper.

3 Place the tracing paper on a blank piece of water-color paper to transfer the image. Rub or sketch over the outline you sketched onto the tracing paper to transfer the pencil on the opposite side onto the paper.

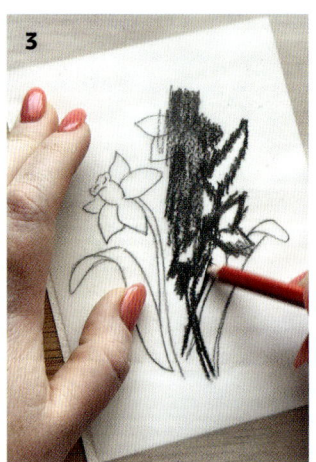

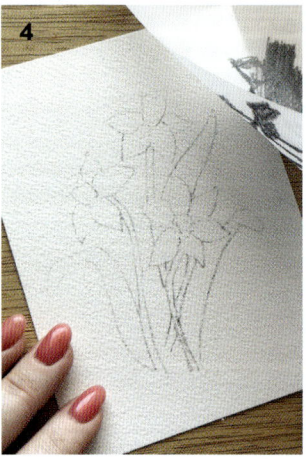

4 When you lift the tracing paper, your sketch will have transferred lightly onto the watercolor paper, perfect for painting flowers on whatever paper you like best!

BASIC WATERCOLOR TECHNIQUES

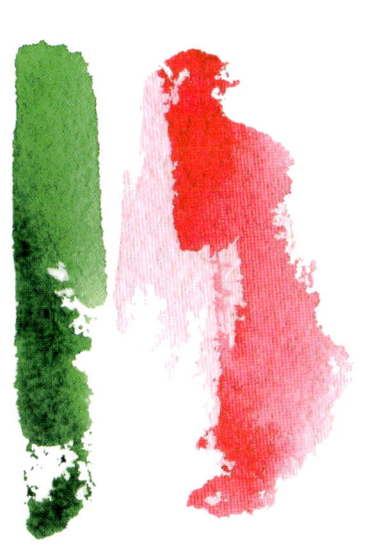

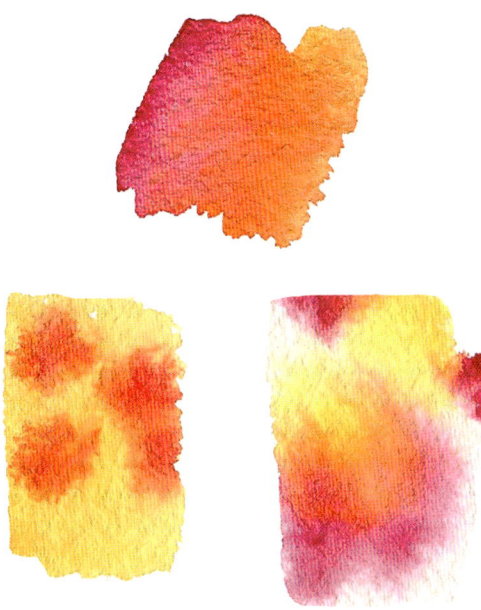

Wet-on-Dry

Wet-on-dry in watercolor refers to applying wet paint onto a dry surface, typically dry paper or a previously painted area. This method allows for more control compared to wet-on-wet, as the paint doesn't spread or blend. Wet-on-dry technique creates sharper edges, defined shapes, and more vibrant colors, as the paint stays more concentrated and doesn't bleed into surrounding areas. It is ideal for adding details, layering colors, or getting crisp lines in a watercolor painting.

Wet-on-Wet

The wet-on-wet technique involves applying wet paint onto a wet surface, allowing the colors to blend and flow into each other. This creates soft, seamless transitions between colors, ideal for gradual blends for the flowers in this book. There are three ways to use this method. First, put two colors side by side while they are wet and let them blend naturally into each other. Second, paint an area with a color and drop another color in for a natural color transition. Third, paint an area with clean water first, and then add colors to blend around the white of the paper. All three ways are important, and we will use them a lot while painting flowers.

Blending

Sometimes with watercolor, you paint a "hard line," but you need the edge to be soft. This is when you use the blending technique. After you apply a stroke of paint, quickly rinse your brush and feather out the edge of the stroke with the clean, damp brush. This will gradually blend the edges and create softer gradients.

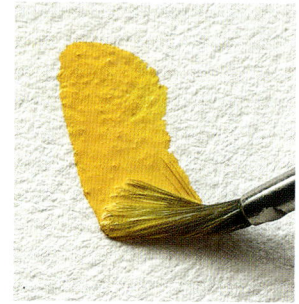 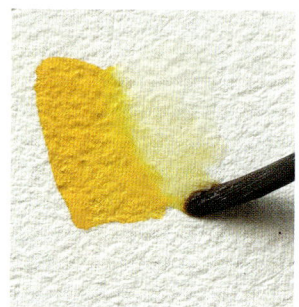

Layering

Transparency is the defining feature of watercolor. Watercolor pigments are suspended in water rather than being mixed with opaque binders like in oil or acrylic paints. This means that each layer of watercolor paint reflects the light and colors underneath it. Because of this, you must start with your lightest layers of watercolor first, preserving those areas as you build up darker layers of detail.

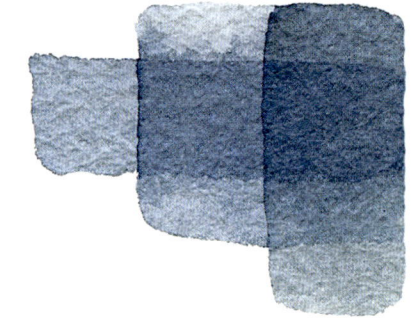

When layering, it's important to make sure that each layer dries completely before adding the next layer, so nothing blends. On the top right, the blue color is the same light wash for all three layers. After the first layer dried, another layer was added, and then another layer after that. You can see that the depth and color have deepened even though the light wash remained the same.

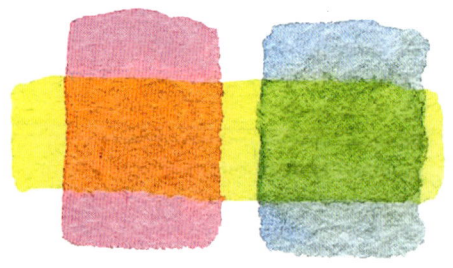

On the middle right, yellow was the first stroke. The yellow was allowed to dry so that the pink and blue did not blend in with the yellow. This glazing effect is a great way to change the color of the paint after it has dried by layering a different color on top. In this case, glazing pink created orange and glazing blue created green.

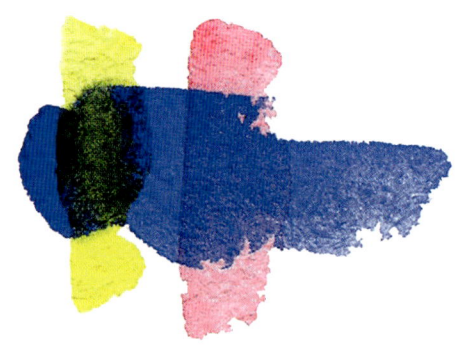

On the bottom right is what happens when you start with a dark swipe of color and try to layer lighter on top. It doesn't work well. You can see that the yellow and pink layered over the top of blue are only bright where there is no blue. So, if you need to paint a light and bright color, you need to paint it first and go around that color with darker paints to preserve it.

Strokes for Flowers

These are the most common ways you will use your brush while painting the flowers in this book. Feel free to practice these strokes on a scrap piece of watercolor before starting the paintings.

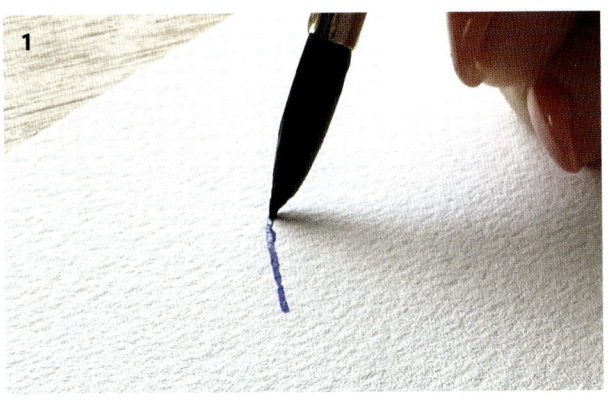

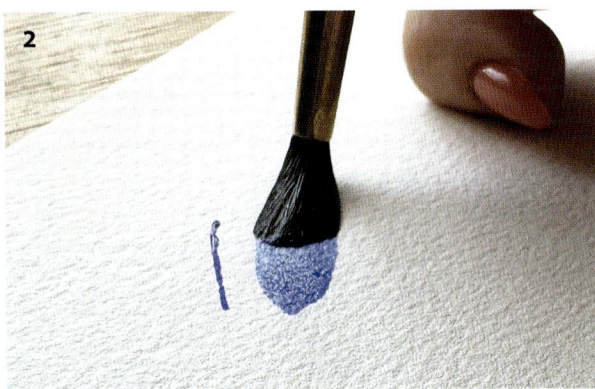

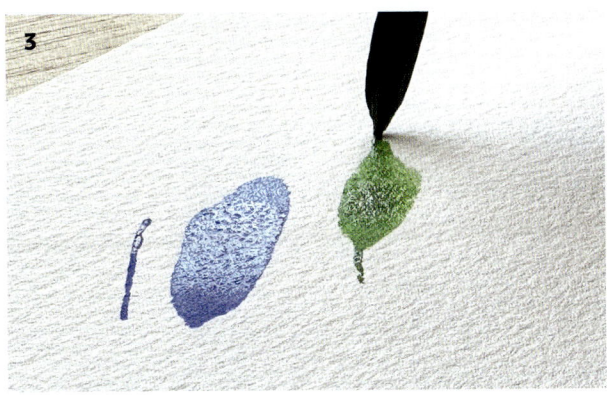

1 Use the very tip of your brush with light pressure and pull your hand to the side while lightly touching the brush to the paper. This will give you a crisp, thin line.

2 Use more pressure to push down on the full body on the brush and pull the brush across the paper for thick, chunky lines.

3 Combining the two will create a lovely leaf shape. Start at the tip of the brush with light pressure and drag slightly. Then transition to the full body of the brush by pushing down with more pressure. Finish by lifting slowly back up to the tip of the brush at the end. This transition from the tip to the body of the brush and back again is a great technique to practice.

4 For large areas, use the body of the brush and swipe up, then down. Repeating this up-and-down sweep creates curvy flower petals.

ALL ABOUT COLOR

Getting comfortable with watercolor takes a basic understanding of color theory. It's a topic that intimidates some newer artists, but I'm here to help! Over the next few pages, you'll see that you can create a vast rainbow of colors with a little bit of color mixing. First, let's look at color value and how to get the level of color saturation you want.

Color Value

Value is how light or dark a color is. In other media, white paint is added to make lighter values and black paint for darker values, but not with watercolor! In watercolor, values are controlled by water. If you want a light color of blue, add more water. If you want a more intense blue, add less water. When we add

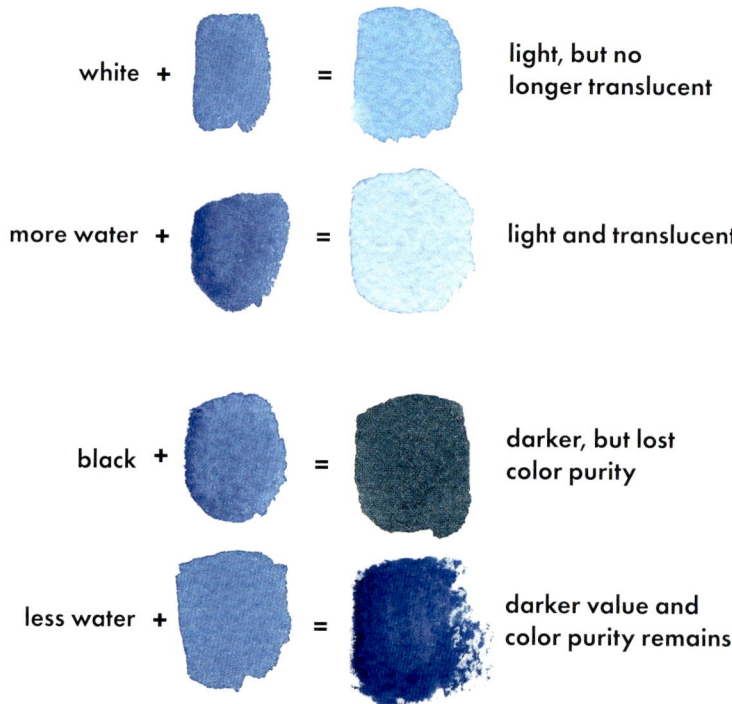

white + = light, but no longer translucent

more water + = light and translucent

black + = darker, but lost color purity

less water + = darker value and color purity remains

TRANSPARENT – OPAQUE

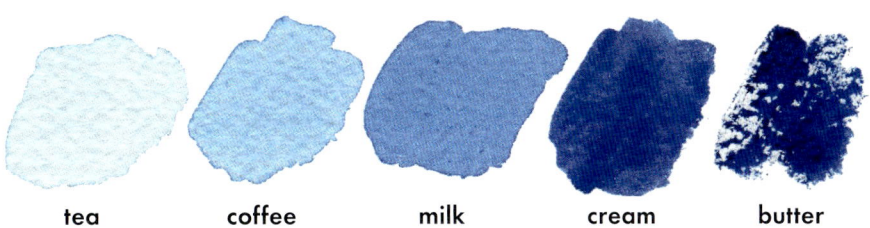

tea coffee milk cream butter

VALUE SCALE

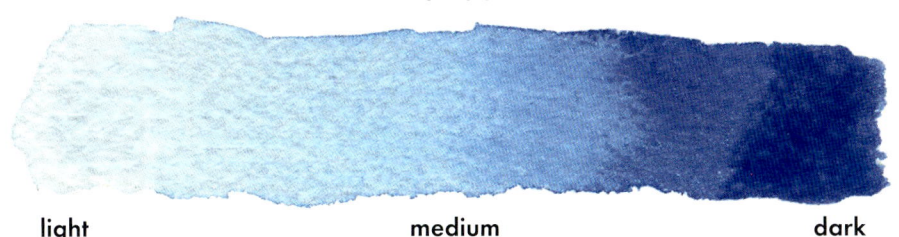

light medium dark

white to watercolor, we lose transparency, and the mixture becomes opaque. This is not necessarily wrong for every situation, but not how we create light, transparent colors. On the other hand, when we add black to watercolor, we change its chroma, or purity of color. It becomes a completely different color instead of a darker version of the same color. To keep the color's purity but increase its darker value, pick up more pigment and less water.

Value Scale

There is a wide range of color value you can achieve by mixing different amounts of water and pigment together. This is called a value scale. You can remember values based on their amount of

transparency, and I like to compare washes to tea, coffee, milk, cream, and butter based on the amount of water and pigment they have. For example, light value washes are more transparent, like tea, and the more pigment you add, the less transparent the wash of color becomes, getting closer to coffee and milk in transparency. Darker value washes are thicker like cream and then butter, less transparent with more pigment, which makes them flow less. Knowing values is the key to watercolor. Start with light values first and then slowly add darker values as you build up color and details. Remember, you can't bring your light areas back, so you need to start with them and paint around them. You'll know you're done with a painting when you have light, medium, and dark values present.

The Color Wheel

PRIMARY COLORS
I follow the cyan, magenta, yellow (CMY) color theory. This color theory uses bright primaries of blue, pink, and yellow to create bright and intense colors with the best nonmuddy purples!

SECONDARY COLORS
When two primary colors are mixed in equal amounts, they create the secondary colors. With the CMY color theory, red, green, and purple become secondary colors on the color wheel. Yellow and pink mixing to produce red might not be what you remember from grade school art class. This is specific to watercolor!

TERTIARY COLORS
Tertiary colors are made when a primary color and a secondary color combine. For example, yellow + green = yellow-green and yellow + red = orange.

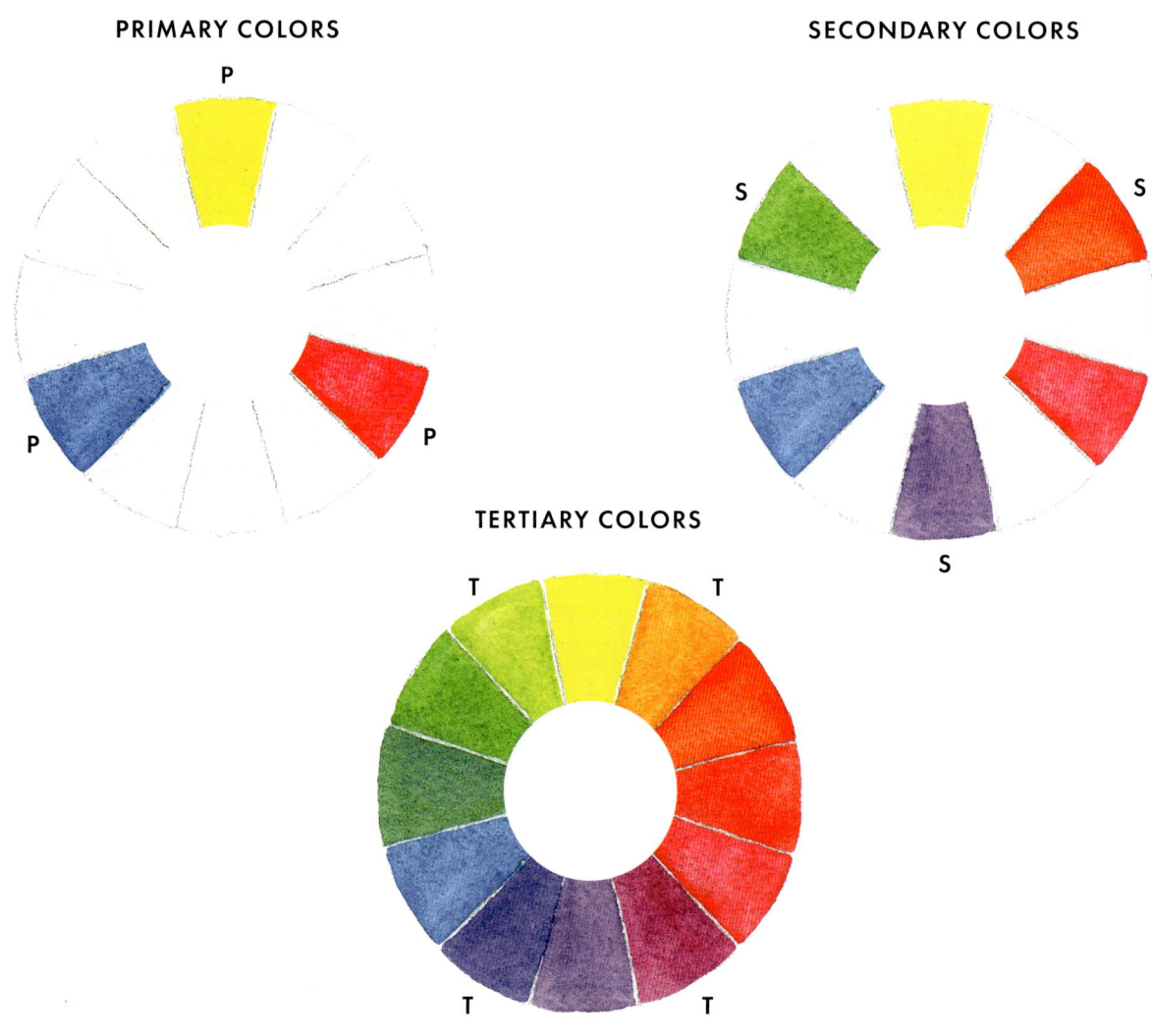

PRIMARY COLORS

SECONDARY COLORS

TERTIARY COLORS

ANALOGOUS COLORS

COMPLEMENTARY COLORS

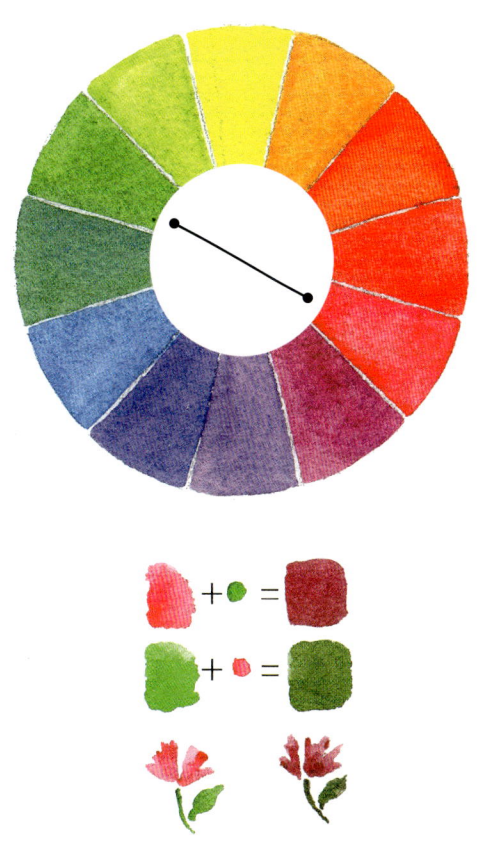

ANALOGOUS COLORS

Analogous colors are colors that are next to each other on the color wheel. These colors typically create harmonious combinations when used together in artwork. For example, orange, red-orange, and red are analogous colors. They blend well to create new colors that are bright in chroma.

COMPLEMENTARY COLORS

Complementary colors are colors that are opposite each other on the color wheel. Red and green, blue and orange, and yellow and purple are examples of complementary color pairs. When used next to each

other, they create high contrast and make each other appear more vibrant. When mixed, complementary colors can neutralize each other, creating grays at an equal mix, or muted colors in smaller amounts.

For example, pink and green are across from each other on the color wheel. I can use these colors to paint a bright flower without mixing them. However, if I mix a tiny bit of green into the pink, I get a muted dusty rose color. If I mix a tiny bit of pink into the green, I get a muted olive green color. You can use your knowledge of complementary colors to create deeper colors for darker values and shadows that appear more natural.

CARNATION

 Permanent rose

 Lemon yellow

 Sap green

 Ultramarine

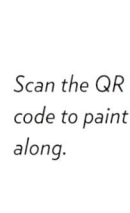 *Scan the QR code to paint along.*

1 **Petal base color:** Pick up permanent rose and add water to your palette until the color is a very light pink. Remember, more water makes light colors without needing to add white. Loosely fill in the petals of the carnations with this light color. Leave some areas of white space around the edges and within the petals; don't fill in every line like a coloring book. This gives the painting room to "breathe" and creates a loose watercolor style.

2 **Petal shadows:** Now you are going to start building up the layers of color and shadow within the carnation. Wait until the first layer is almost dry so that you get a slight bleed without the second color overtaking the light pink. Use a little more permanent rose in your mix to get a slightly darker color without adding any other colors. Make sure to place this second, slightly more pigmented color of permanent rose right at the base of the petals. Remember that a flower is like a cone, and the colors will be darker and more in shadow as the bottom of the petal attaches to the stem. Also, add this color where the petals overlap, causing additional shadows.

3 **Deeper petal shadows:** As the layers dry, add an additional layer of shadow that has harder lines. For this color you are still using only permanent rose but adding slightly

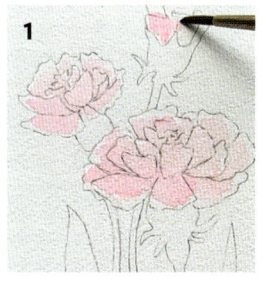

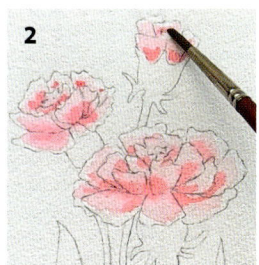

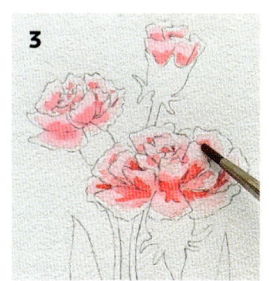

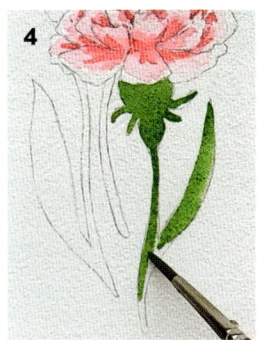

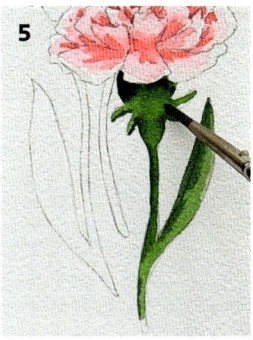

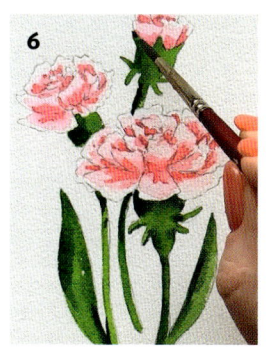

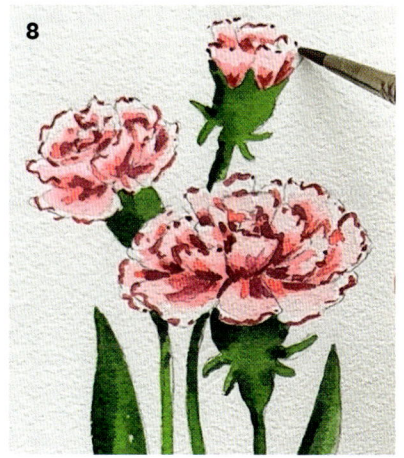

5. **Greenery shadows:** Use more sap green and add some ultramarine to get a deep green mixture. Add this darker blue green to the base green color while it's still wet to get a blended shadow. Focus this color on the shadowy areas. A little bit goes a long way.

6. **More greenery shadows:** Using the lemon yellow and sap green mixture, fill in the rest of the greenery with a medium wash. Adding more sap green and ultramarine to the mixture, tap this deeper color into the base green while it's still wet to create shadowy blends.

7. **Deeper petal shadows:** Mix permanent rose and ultramarine to get a deep purple for the petal shadows. Lean more into the permanent rose so that the color is still pink, but deeper. Place this color minimally and right at the base of petals and in the overlapped petal shadow areas. Use this same mix, permanent rose and ultramarine, to add loose wavy lines at the tips of the petals. This helps define the petals, especially the ones that are kind of "lost" in the center of the flower.

more pigment to your mixture to get a more intense color. You need less of this color, so keep it close to the base of the petals without painting over too much of the washes that came before.

4. **Greenery base color:** Mix the lemon yellow and sap green to get the base color for all the greenery. This is a medium wash mixture with an equal amount of water and pigment. You need to apply a darker color while this color is still wet, so paint one section of greenery at a time.

8. **Petal outlines:** Using the deeper petal color, add squiggly lines around the tips of the petals. Leave the white space that you created at the beginning for breathing room. You don't have to connect every line. Implied lines have a major effect on loose watercolor style.

JANUARY
SNOWDROP

 Permanent rose

 Ultramarine

 Sap green

 Cadmium-free yellow

 Lemon yellow

 Burnt sienna

 *Scan the QR code to paint along.*

1 **Paint "white" petals:** Since you don't use white paint with watercolor, you must figure out how to paint "white" using color. I used a mix of permanent rose, ultramarine, sap green, and cadmium-free yellow. The colors opposite on the color wheel help create a dusty blue-gray color with a lot of dimension. Use a lot of water so that this color is very light. You don't want the petals to look like they are gray.

2 **Greenery base color:** Use a mixture of lemon yellow and sap green to create the color for the base color of the greenery. Make sure it's a light enough wash by adding water so you aren't starting with too dark of a value. Mix sap green and ultramarine into your green mixture and add this darker color into the shadowy areas of the greenery. It's okay if your paper has dried; a hardline shadow works well with this long greenery.

3 **Dirt:** Pick up some burnt sienna for a light dirt color. Mix it slightly into the green on the palette to mute the red in the color just a bit. Using your brush almost parallel to the paper, use a dry brushstroke to get a textured, grainy look for the dirt. Make sure to leave gaps of white paper for the "snow" on the ground as well. Add a bit of ultramarine to the burnt sienna mixture to get a deep brown color. Tap this color in while the light dirt

color is still wet. Focus this color at the base of the snow patches to look like shadow.

4 **Petal shadows:** Using a very light wash of ultramarine, add shadows to the white petals. Pick a side where your light source is coming from and paint the shadows on the opposite side consistently throughout the painting. If you ever put a stroke with too much blue in it, rinse your brush and blend the color out with water. You still want to give the impression that these are white petals.

5 **Greenery shadows:** Mix sap green, ultramarine, and permanent rose to get a deep green color for an extra contrast in the greenery. Add this minimally around the shadowy areas of the greenery. Make sure not to overpower the middle green shadow so you get a nice, layered look between light, medium, and dark values present in the greens. Two of the flowers have the center showing. Add some lemon yellow to the green mixture to get a warmer deep green. Place a little line between the flower petals at that center edge.

6 **Inner shadows:** Using the shadow colors you already mixed on your palette, place a little bit of shadow where the petals meet on the two flowers where you can see the centers. Focus this color at the top and away from the green tip you added to the center already.

7 **More shadows:** Now that the petals are completely dry, add one last bit of shadow for contrast. Using the ultramarine shadow color already mixed on the palette, place more concentrated color but only in a few areas. Remember to place it on the same side as the rest of your petal shadows to be consistent with your light source.

8 **Yellow pop of color:** Finish off the painting with a pop of lemon yellow right where the flower connects to the stem.

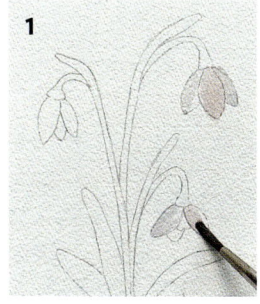
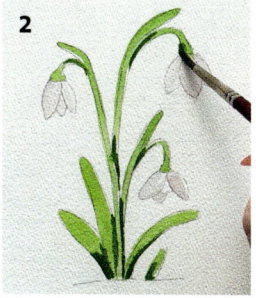
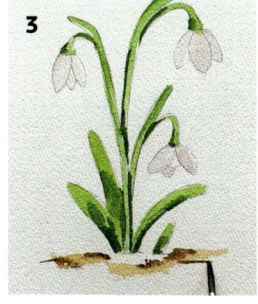
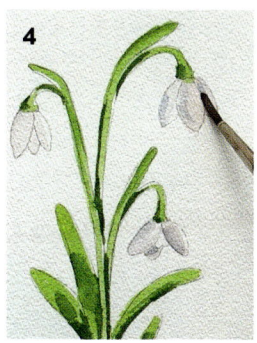
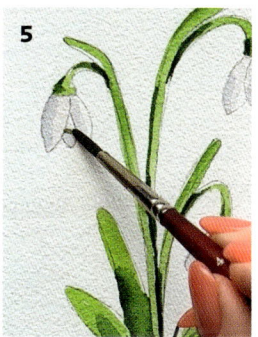
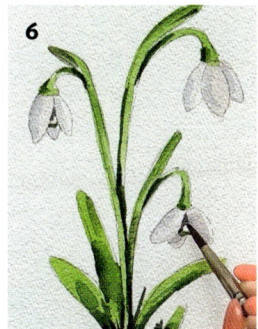
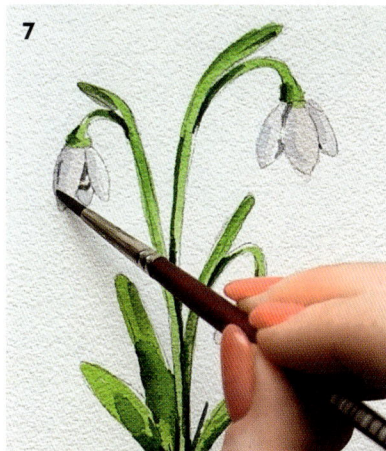
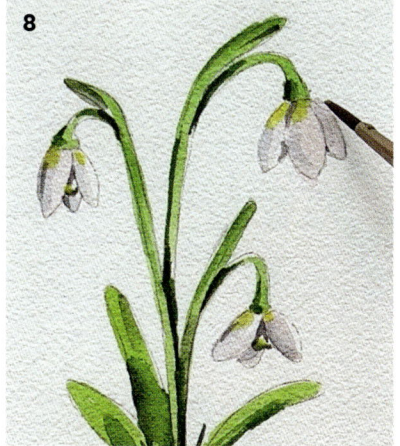

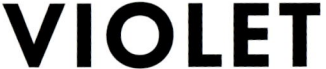

VIOLET

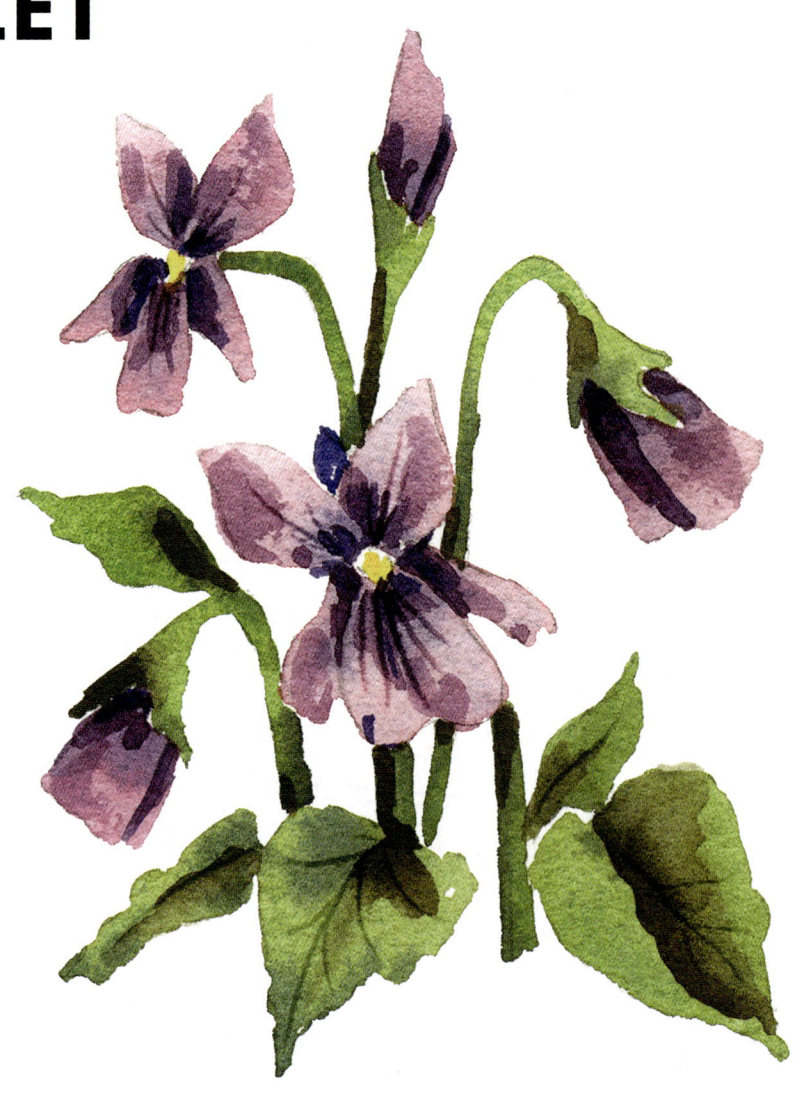

 Permanent rose

 Cerulean

 Ultramarine

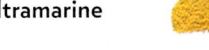 **Lemon yellow**

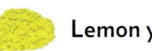 **Cadmium-free yellow**

Scan the QR code to paint along.

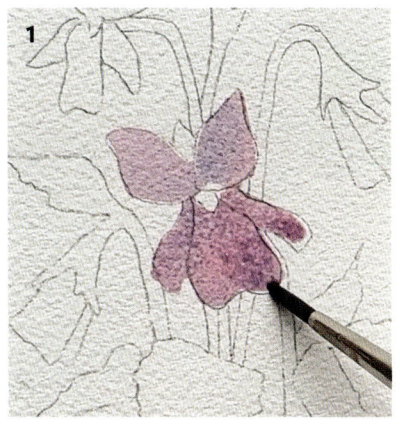
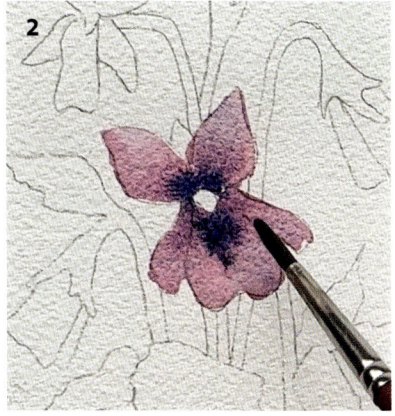
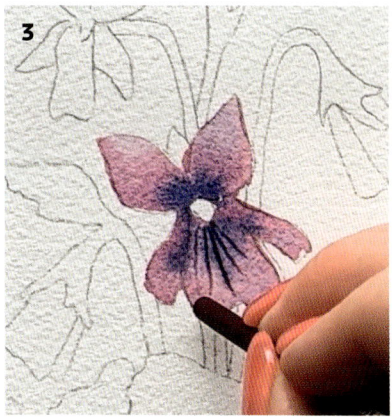
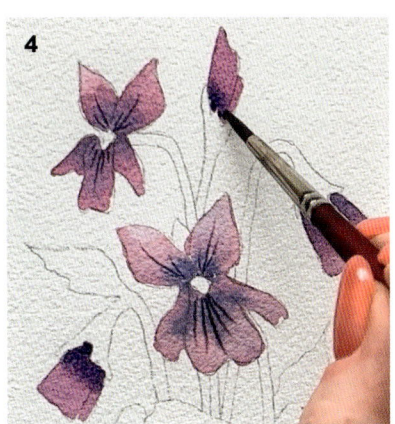
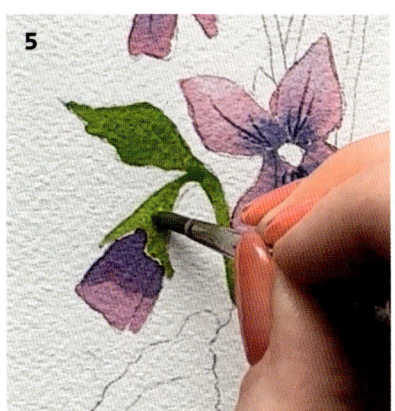
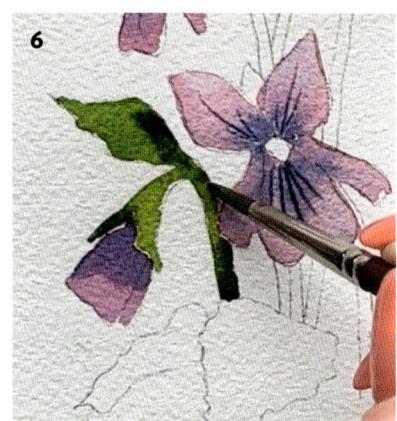

1 **Petal base color:** Mix permanent rose and cerulean to get a light lavender color. Add water so that the wash is light. Apply to the petals one flower at a time so that the flower stays wet for the next step. Keep the center open.

2 **Petal shadows:** While the base lavender wash is still wet, mix ultramarine into the mixture on the palette to get a deep blue purple. Add this color around the center of the flower, letting the colors bleed. Move quickly to the next step.

3 **Flower veins:** While the petals are still wet, flip your brush around. Using the hard, more pointed end of your brush, push slightly into the paper and drag from the flower center out toward the end of the petals. This creates a light impression in the paper, allowing pigment to flow in and create a natural-looking darker line that can be more precise than painting it with your brush.

4 **Flower buds:** Repeat the first three steps on the rest of the flowers. For the flower buds, focus the deeper purple color at the end of the petals where they meet the stem.

5 **Greenery base color:** Mix lemon yellow, cadmium-free yellow, and cerulean to get a bright warm green. Add this color to the greenery, working in sections to keep the base layer wet.

6 **Greenery shadows:** Add ultramarine to the green mixture to get a deep blue green color. Tap this color into the base green already applied while it's still wet to get a natural-looking shadow bleed.

7 **Veins in leaves:** For the large leaves, apply the green in the same way as other greenery, but immediately after you apply the dark green, press the back of the brush into the paper to create the veins. This is the same technique used earlier on the petals, just with a different pattern for leaves.

8 **Yellow centers:** Add a pop of cadmium-free yellow to the center of each flower.

9 **Layered shadows:** Mix permanent rose and ultramarine to create a deep purple color for the petal shadows. Apply this color when everything is dry for hard lines. Focus this color where the petals overlap and there would be a natural shadow. On the flower buds, add the shadow color at the line where the petals are wrapped around each other.

10 **Deeper greenery shadows:** Mix cadmium-free yellow, ultramarine, a bit of permanent rose, and cerulean for a dark green color. Apply this color at the base of the stems, where the flowers meet the greenery, and the folds and centers of the leaves for shadows in the greenery.

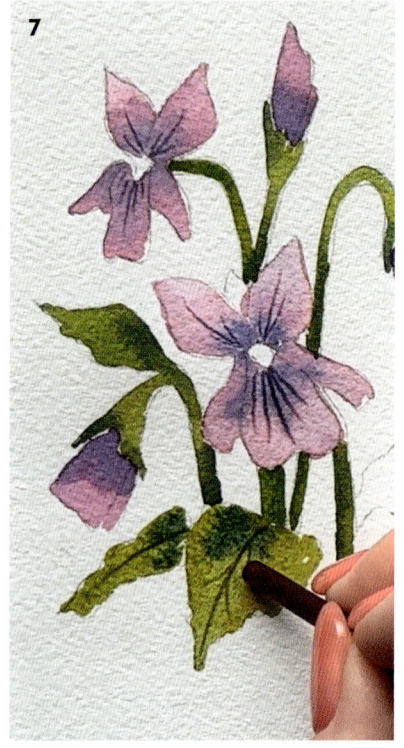

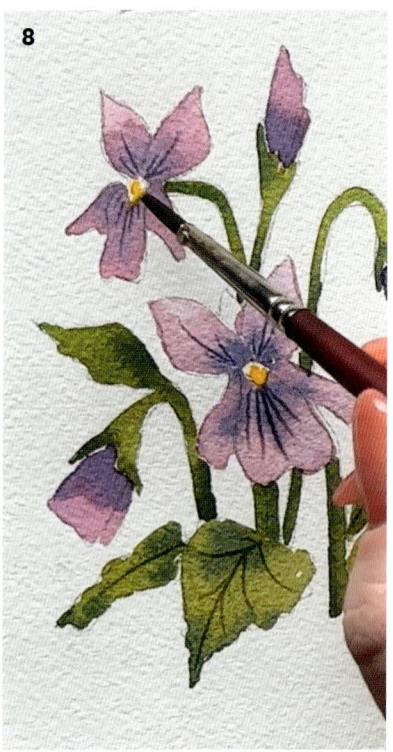

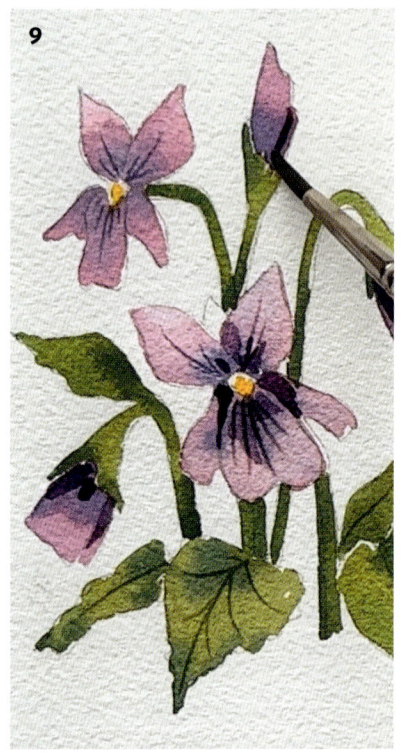

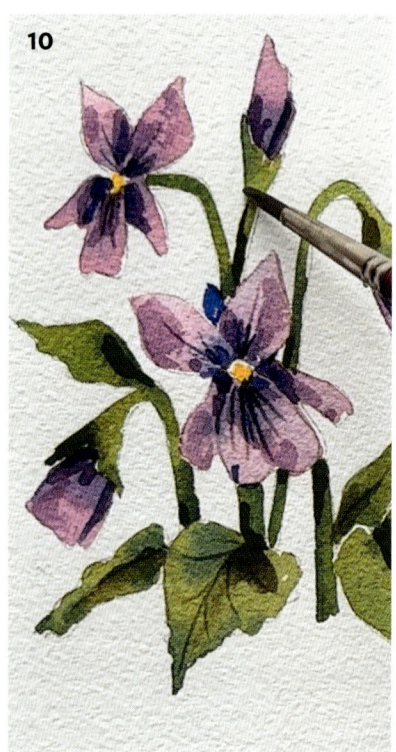

PRIMROSE

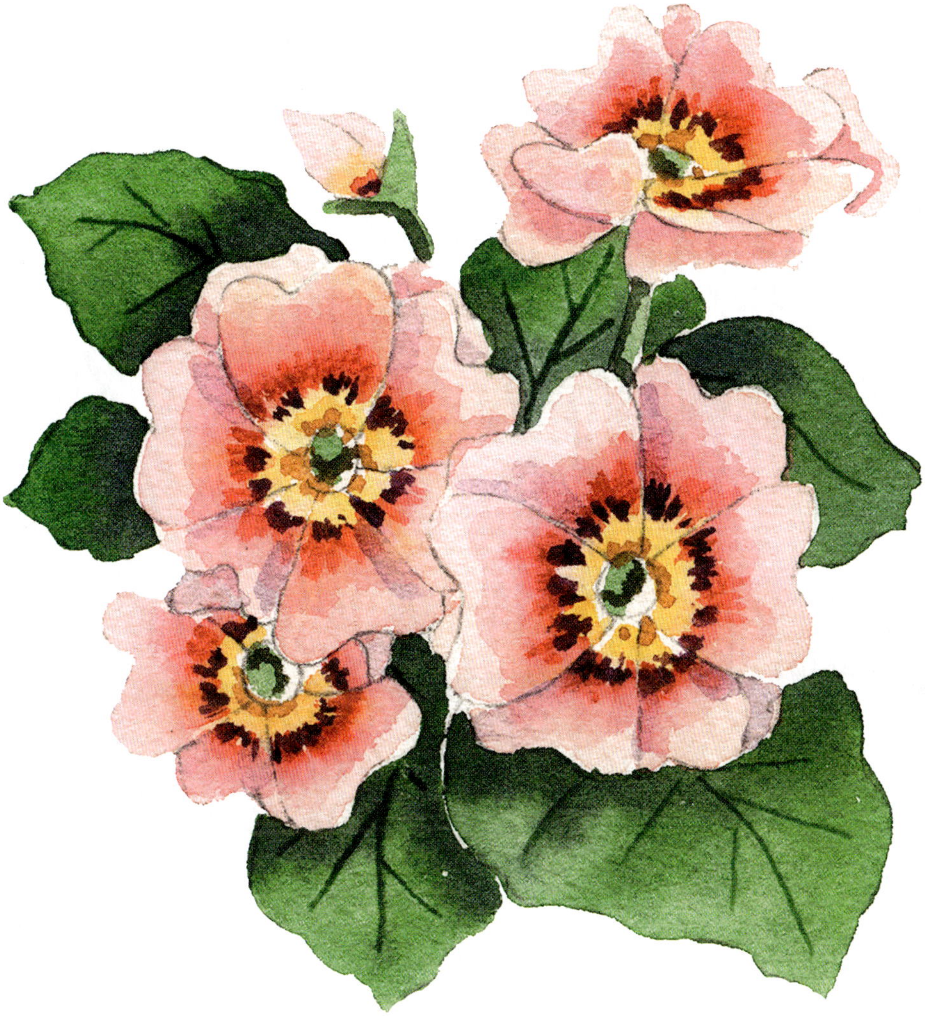

 Cadmium-free yellow

 Sap green

 Cadmium-free red

 Permanent rose

 Ultramarine

Scan the QR code to paint along.

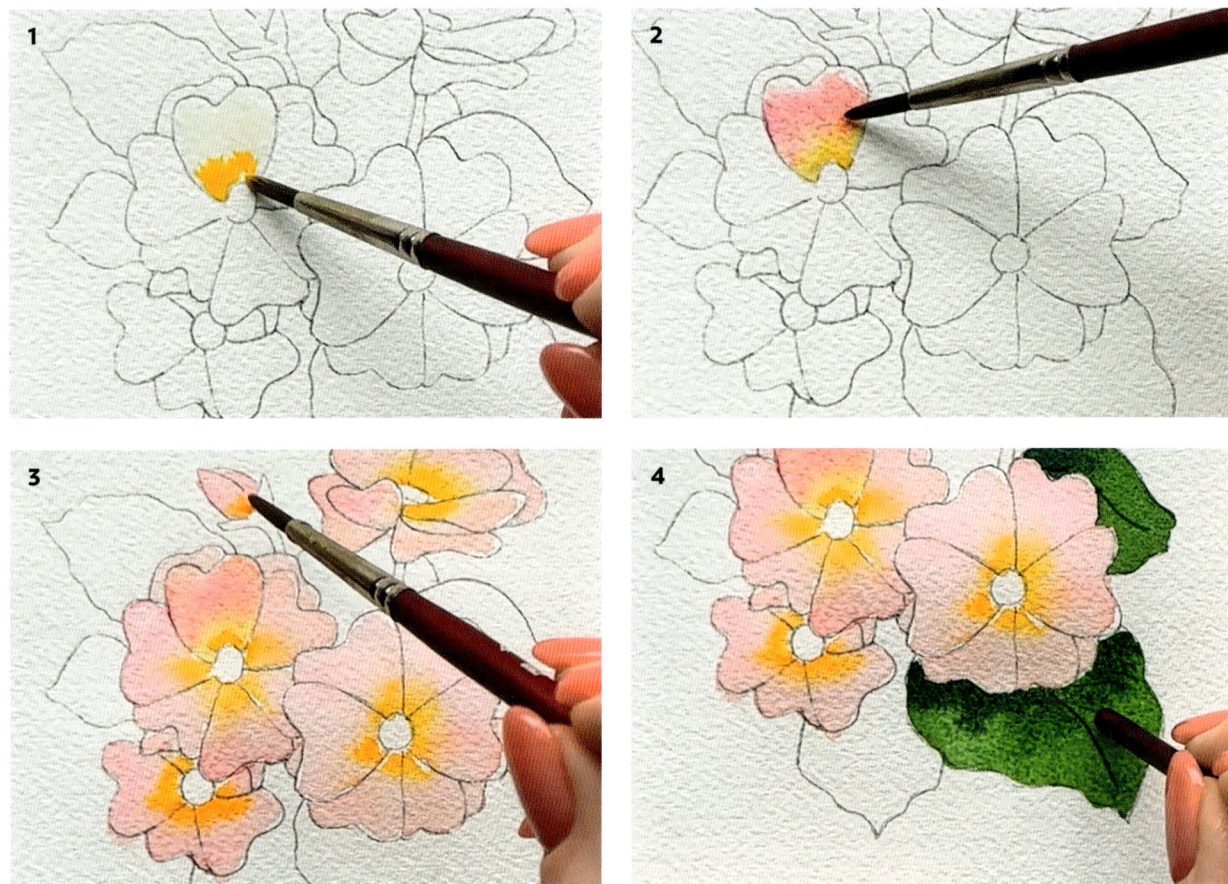

1 **Yellow petal color:** Paint one heart-shaped petal with clean water. Tap cadmium-free yellow into the water at the base of the petal near the center. Rinse and dry your brush. With a damp brush, lightly blend the yellow into the watery areas while keeping the color concentrated at the center.

2 **Pink petal color:** Pick up a light wash of permanent rose and add that above the yellow into the wet petal. Rinse and tap the water out of your brush. With a damp brush, blend the pink and yellow together until you get a nice soft blend.

3 **Repeat for remaining petals:** Repeat steps 1 and 2 on each petal one at a time until you have painted all the flowers. This will help keep your petals from drying before you can add in wet-on-wet details.

4 **Greenery base color:** Mix sap green with a bit of ultramarine and add this color to the leaves. While this color is still wet, add more ultramarine to your mix on the palette and drop this deep shadow color at the base of the leaf under the flower. Moving quickly, use the hard end of your brush to gently press into the paper and drag from the base of the leaf near the flower to the end of the leaf, creating leaf veins. The slight pressure in the paper creates an indentation and the pigment flow into it, creating a dark, natural-looking line. Repeat for all the leaves.

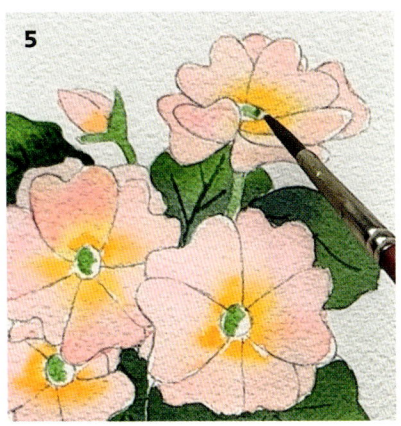

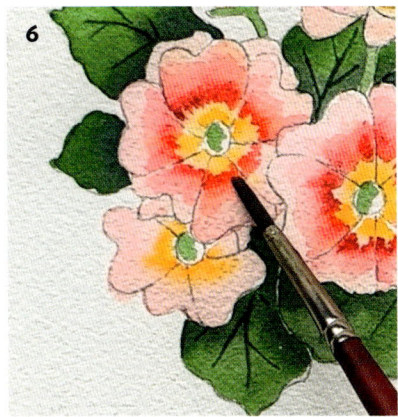

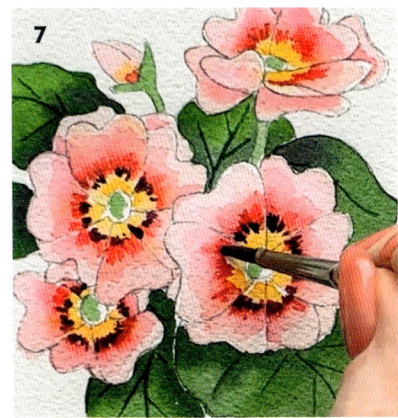

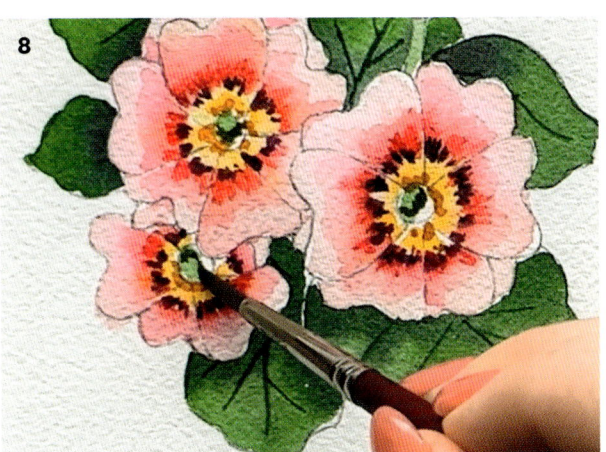

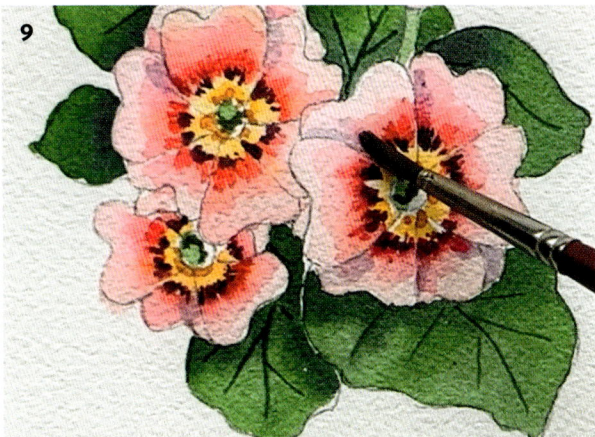

5 Green flower centers: Pick up the bright light green on your palette and add it to the centers of all the flowers. Leave a little bit of white space for breathing room.

6 Pink details: Pick up a much more concentrated wash of permanent rose for the details in the petals. Paint the color on thick at first right where the pink and the yellow meet, creating an uneven line. Rinse your brush and then with water blend the outer edge up into the pink, keeping the line at the yellow a hard edge. Do this on all the petals. Work in sections so the magenta doesn't dry before you have the chance to blend it out.

7 Dark pink details: Mix permanent rose and ultramarine to get a deep purple that leans more magenta. Place this color lightly right where the yellow and the pink meet on the petals. The lines should be uneven, disconnected, and small. Repeat on all petals.

8 Adding contrast: Mix cadmium-free yellow with a touch of cadmium-free red to get a deep golden orange color. Add this color around the centers in the yellow section. Pick up some of the deep green used on the leaves earlier and add a small swipe of this color to the very center to give some contrast with the bright green.

9 Petal shadows: Add a very light wash of ultramarine around the petals where they naturally overlap. This creates a light shadow with the ultramarine wash acting as a glaze.

MARCH

DAFFODIL

 Cadmium-free yellow

 Cadmium-free red

 Lemon yellow

 Cerulean

 Ultramarine

 *Scan the QR code to paint along.*

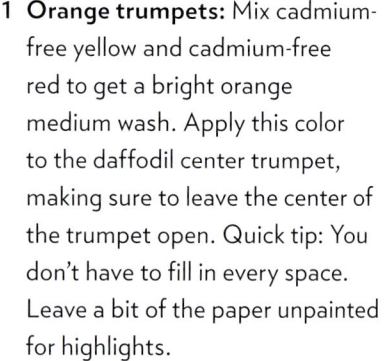

1 **Orange trumpets:** Mix cadmium-free yellow and cadmium-free red to get a bright orange medium wash. Apply this color to the daffodil center trumpet, making sure to leave the center of the trumpet open. Quick tip: You don't have to fill in every space. Leave a bit of the paper unpainted for highlights.

2 **Yellow petals:** While the orange on the trumpet is still wet, pick up a medium wash mix of both yellows: cadmium-free yellow and lemon yellow. Tap the brush to the center trumpet and pull the stroke out through the petal shape to paint the petals. This will allow some blending of the trumpet color into the petals. Use this same technique for all three blooms.

3 **Greenery base color:** Mix lemon yellow and cadmium-free yellow with cerulean and ultramarine until you get a light wash of warm green. Remember, you are starting with your lightest values of green first. Add this mix to all the stems and leaves. Mix ultramarine into the green mixture to create a deep blue green. Add this color to the bottom of the leaves in shadow areas.

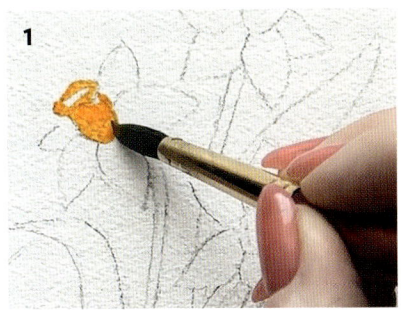

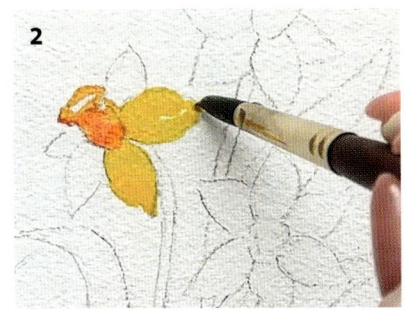

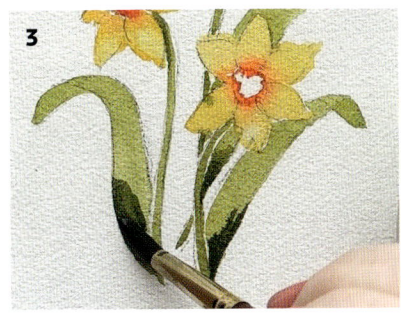

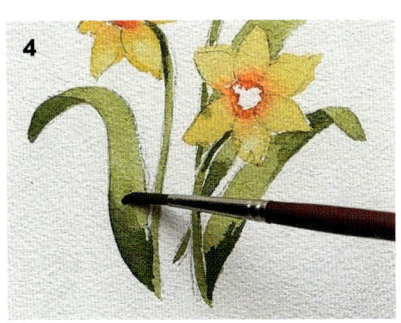

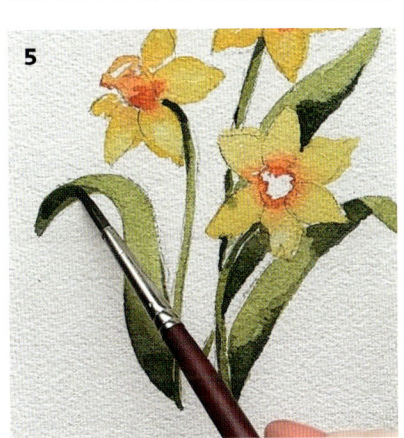

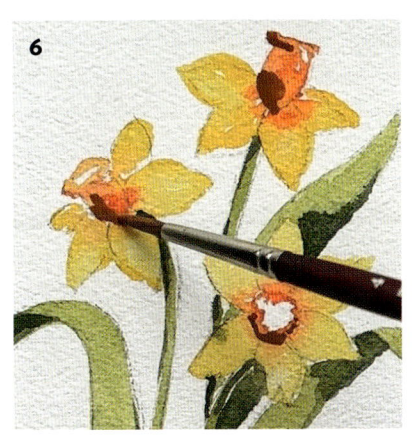

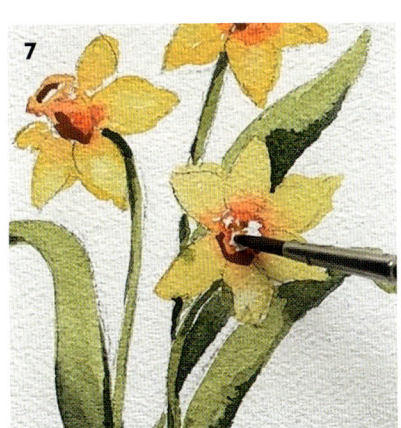

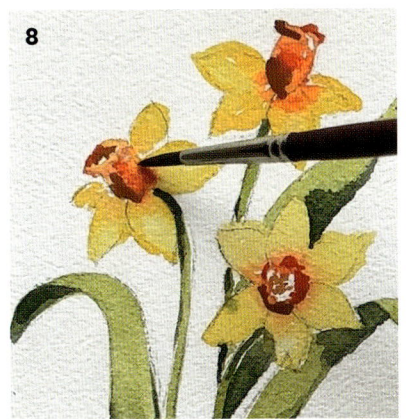

4 **Greenery shadows:** Add the same ultramarine-green mix under the angled part of the leaves to create the shadows as the leaf is curving over. Use water to blend out any harsh shadow lines that you want to soften.

5 **Deeper greenery shadows:** As the green shadows dry, add another layer of the blue-green mixture to darken the shadows while leaving some of the first two bottom layers showing. You want to see light, medium, and dark values on the leaves.

6 **Trumpet shadows:** Mix a tiny bit of green into the reddish orange mixture you painted the trumpets with. This should create a deep, muddy red. Add this color lightly around the trumpet edges to create a shadow in a few spots. Use the same shadowy red color to paint a shadow on the side of the trumpet as well. A little bit goes a long way, so don't overpower your other colors with this deep color.

7 **Stamens:** Add some small yellow-orange dots to the center of the open daffodil.

8 **Trumpet glaze:** Add a final glaze in a light red-orange wash to bring a pop of color to areas on the trumpet head that need more vibrancy.

CHERRY BLOSSOM

 Permanent rose

 Burnt sienna

 Ultramarine

 Cadmium-free yellow

 Cerulean

 *Scan the QR code to paint along.*

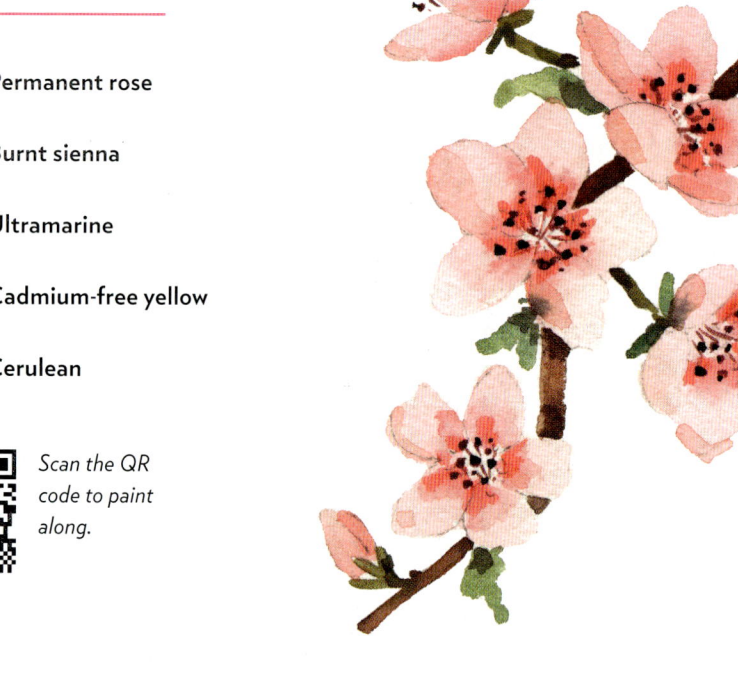

1 **Pink petals:** Pick up some permanent rose and add water to make a very light pink color. Paint a few flowers with this pink color and then move quickly to the next step.

2 **Darker pink centers:** Pick up more concentrated permanent rose and tap this color into the petals around the centers while the light pink layer is still wet.

Repeat these two steps on all flowers. Make sure you keep in mind the flowers that have petals blocking the center or flowers that have no center showing at all.

3 **Brown branch:** Mix burnt sienna, permanent rose, ultramarine, and cadmium-free yellow to get a brown color for the branch. Add water to the mixture to make sure it is a light wash. Place this

color along the branch in sections and add extra ultramarine in a few places for dimension while everything is still wet.

4 **Greenery base color:** Mix cadmium-free yellow and cerulean to get a bright light green. Add green stems from the flowers to the main brown branch. It's nice if they bleed a bit into the brown stem, but it looks great as a hard

line too. Repeat the process of adding the brown color, darker ultramarine details, and smaller green stems to the rest of the branch. Make sure that you bring the bright green color up and around the buds when you paint their stems. The main star is the flowers, so don't go overboard with the leaves. Add a few here and there using the same light green wash as the stems. Use the shape of your brush to push down and create small irregular shapes that give the impression of leaves.

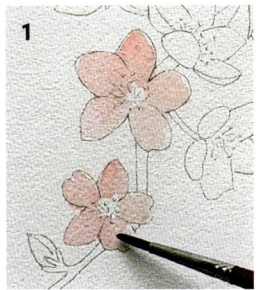
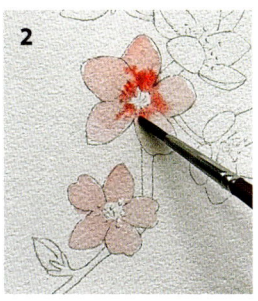
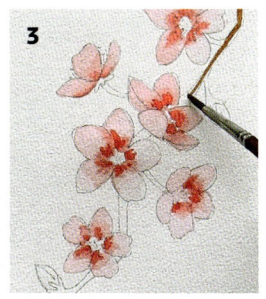
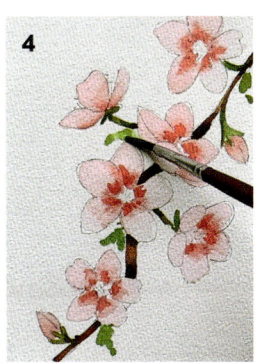
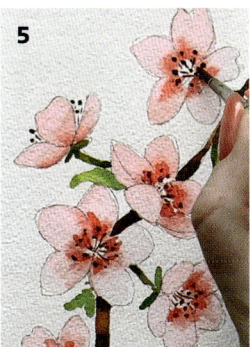
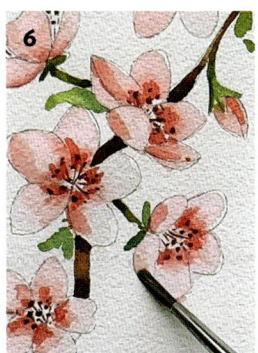
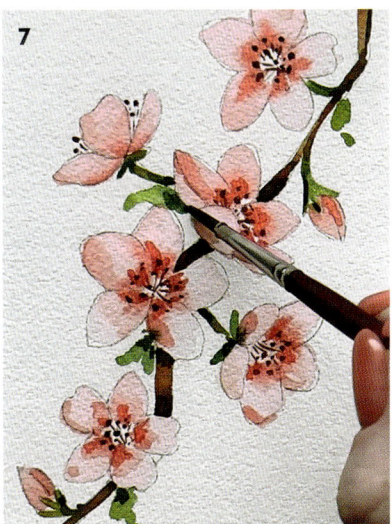
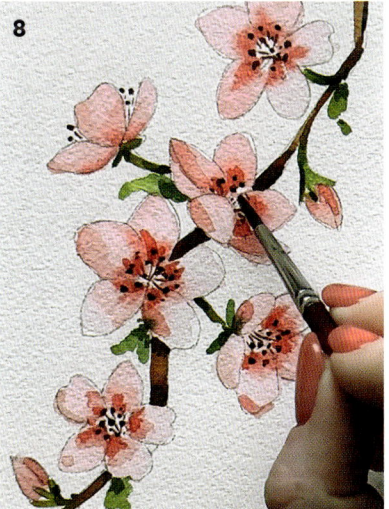

5   **Stamens:** Mix permanent rose with a bit of cerulean to get a deeper purple color. Add dots in varying sizes and heights to the middle of the flower to create the tips of the stamen. Add a bit of ultramarine to the deep purple mixture to get a slightly deeper color. Use this color and the very tip of your brush with light pressure to create the small lines that connect the dots to the flower. Slightly curve them depending on the direction they are going.

6   **Petal shadows:** Add water to permanent rose to get a light wash for a glaze. Add this color around the petals for a bit more depth, focusing on the overlapping areas where there would be a natural shadow.

7   **Greenery shadows:** Add a bit more ultramarine to the greens on your palette to create a deep blue green. Place this color on the leaves and stems where they attach to the branch or are tucked under a flower.

8   **Stamen contrast:** To the purple mix on your palette, add a lot more ultramarine to get a deep, dark purple. Use this color to add more contrast to the center stamen and filaments at the end.

DAISY

 Cadmium-free yellow

 Ultramarine

 Cadmium-free red

 Lemon yellow

 Sap green

 Burnt sienna

 Permanent rose

 *Scan the QR code to paint along.*

1 **Yellow centers:** Fill the centers with medium wash of cadmium-free yellow. Move quickly to the next step while the center is still wet.

2 **Petal "white" color:** Mix ultramarine and cadmium-free red using a lot of water. Use light colors to paint "white" without using white paint. Touch the color into the center of the flower while the yellow is still wet and drag out to create the petal using the shape of the brush.

Pick up different colors of light wash to get a variety of colors to create dimension in the petals. Repeat for all the flower petals. Let the colors touch and blend.

3 **Greenery base color:** Mix lemon yellow and sap green to create light bright green for the base color of the greenery and fill in all the greenery with this color. Move quicky to the next step while it's still wet.

4 **Greenery shadows:** Mix more sap green into the green mixture on your palette to create a deeper darker green color. Tap that color into the wet base green color to create natural shadowy blends. Now add ultramarine to the green mixture and tap that into the shadows as well. As your paper starts to dry, the bleeds will become more focused on the areas that you place them, so you'll see light, medium, and dark values in your bleeds while everything is still wet.

5 **Center shadows:** Mix lemon yellow and burnt sienna to create a deep yellow color for the shadow in the center of the flower. Focus the shadows on one side, stippling the color into the center to create texture. Keep the shadow consistent between both flowers.

Add more burnt sienna, sap green, and a bit of ultramarine to the deep yellow color on your palette to create a very deep shadow color for the center. Keep the color focused on the very far side of the shadow area to create light, medium, and dark values for dimension. Dot the color in to create texture.

6 **Petal shadows:** Mix permanent rose and ultramarine with water to get a light shadowy color for the flower petals. Start from the center of the flower going up, adding shadows on the sides where the petals overlap to create naturally dark areas. Increase shadows on the petals as everything begins to dry using light washes of ultramarine, especially on the shadowy side of your flower. Making white flowers look white by using color is all about utilizing the shadows and keeping the highlighted areas bright.

7 **Final center detail:** Pick up more of the dark shadow color from step 5 and add another layer to the shadow side of the center for a final bit of contrast. Keep the texture heavy, stippling it lightly into the center while keeping most of it along the side.

8 **Deeper greenery shadows:** Mix ultramarine into the green mix on your palette to create a deep green for the final shadow details on the greenery. Focus the color on the shadow side of the flower and remember that less is more with the final contrasting colors.

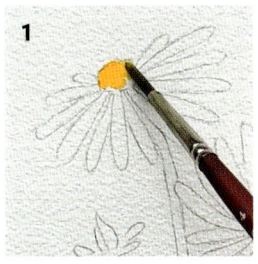
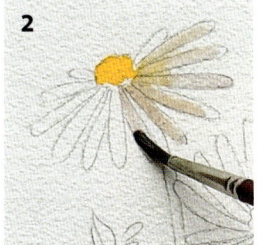
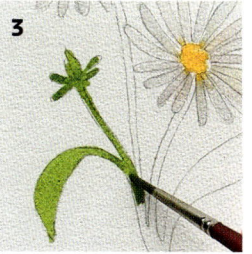
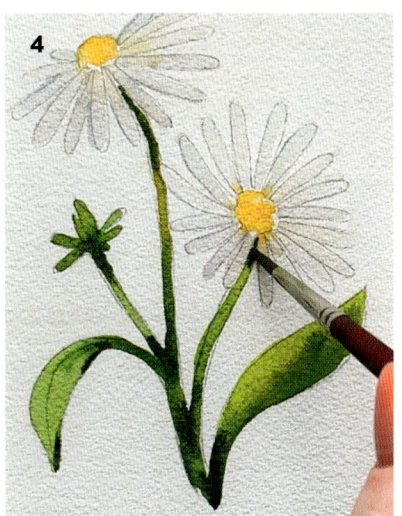
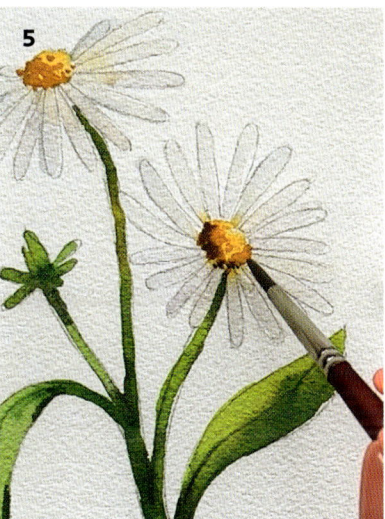
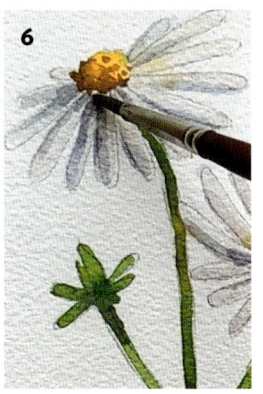
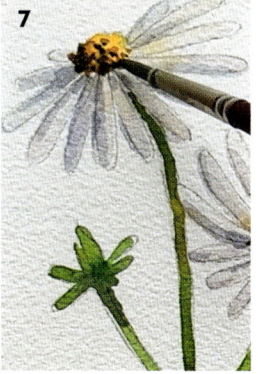
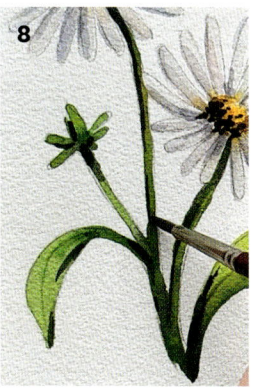

SWEET PEA

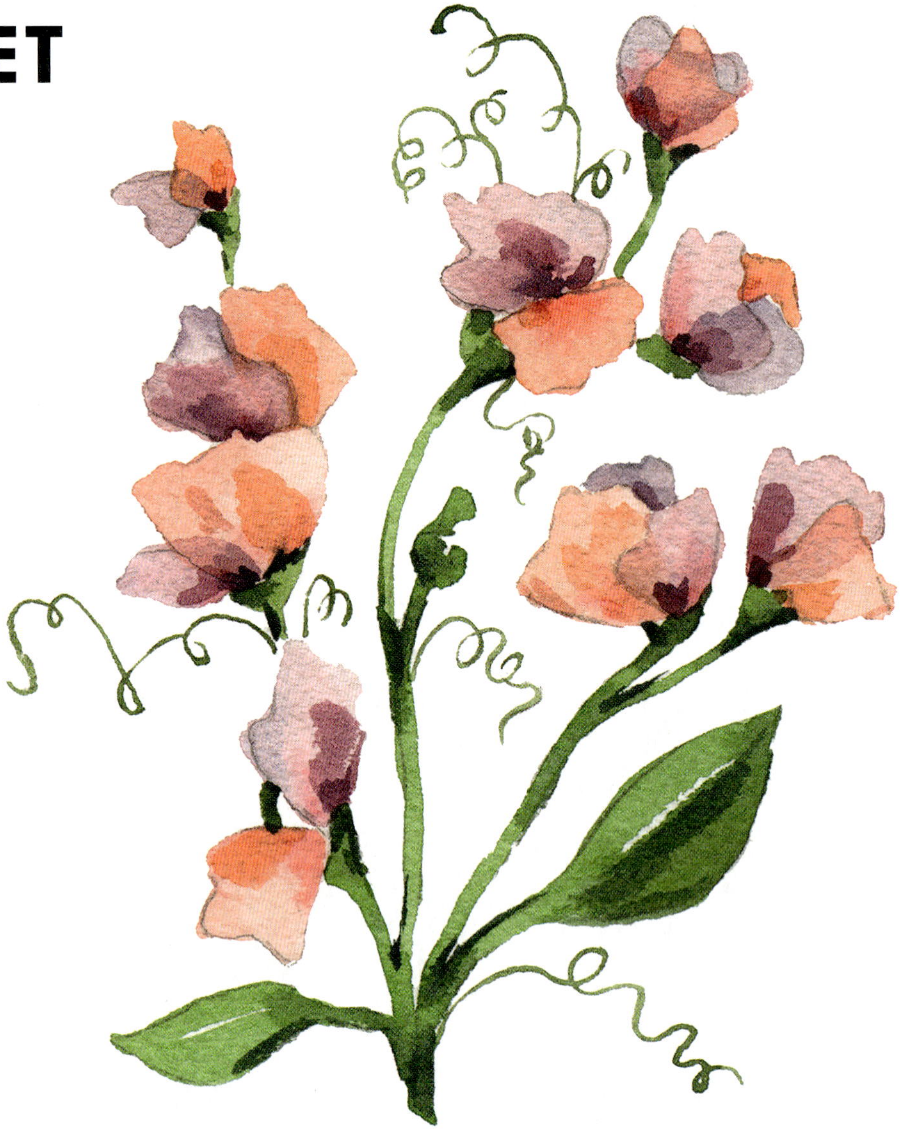

 Permanent rose

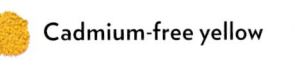 Cadmium-free yellow

 Cerulean

 Lemon yellow

 Sap green

 Ultramarine

Scan the QR code to paint along.

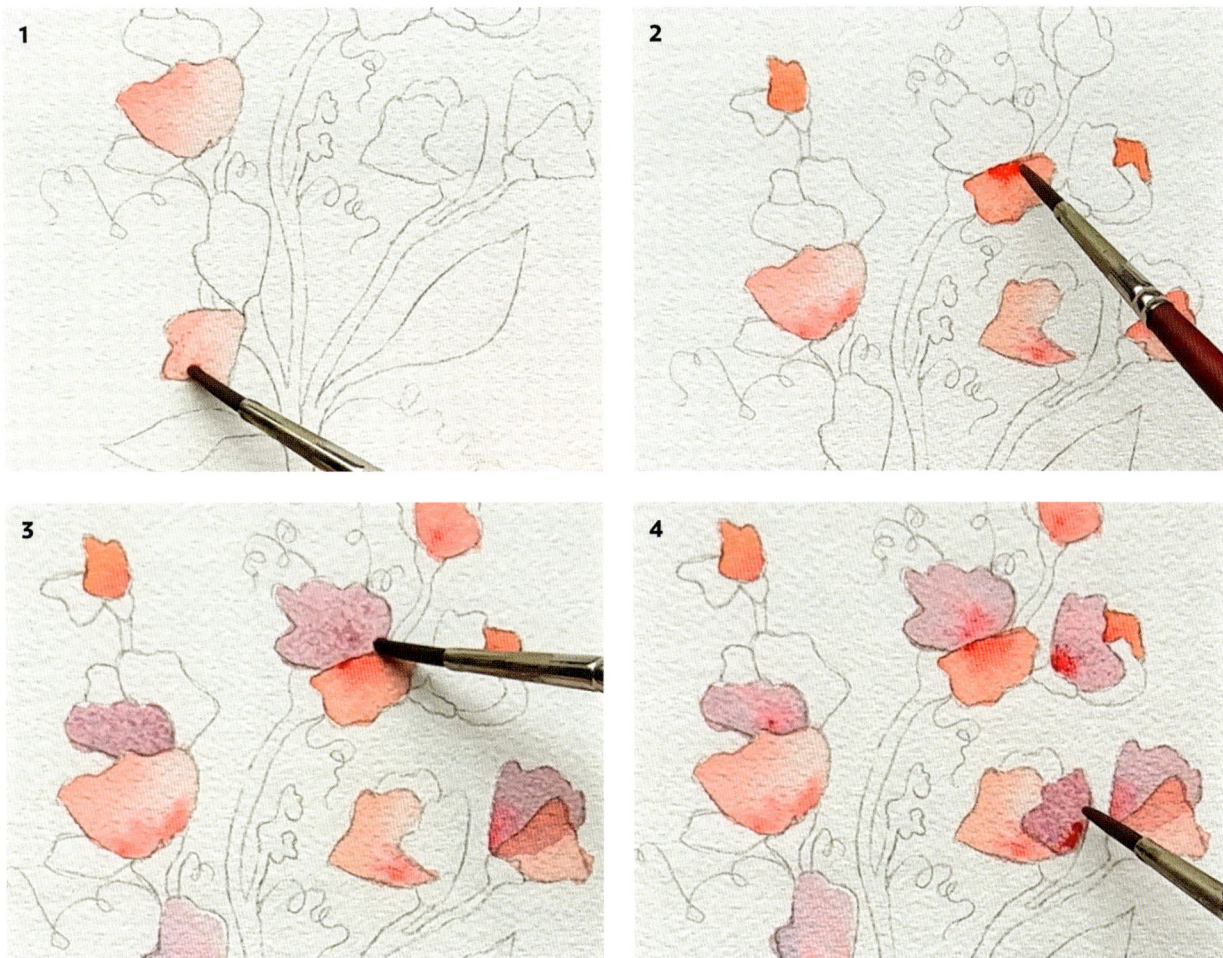

1 **Pink petal base:** Add lots of water to a mix of permanent rose with a bit of cadmium-free yellow for a pale pink color. Fill in one or two petals on each flower. Move quickly to the next step.

2 **Pink petal shadow:** While the base color is still wet, pick up a more pigmented wash of permanent rose and tap it into the flower either at the base where the flower attaches to the stem or where the petal leads into the center of the flower.

3 **Purple petal base:** Mix permanent rose and cerulean to create a light purple color. This should also be a light wash so that if you layer this petal over the top of a pink petal, you can see the petal underneath. Fill in the other petals on the flowers, overlapping when you can. Move quickly to the next step while everything is still wet.

4 **Purple petal shadow:** While the purple base is still wet, pick up a more pigmented wash of permanent rose and tap it into the flower either at the base where the flower attaches to the stem or where the petal leads into the center of the flower. Fill in any remaining petals with either the pink or purple light washes, overlapping some when the petals underneath are completely dry.

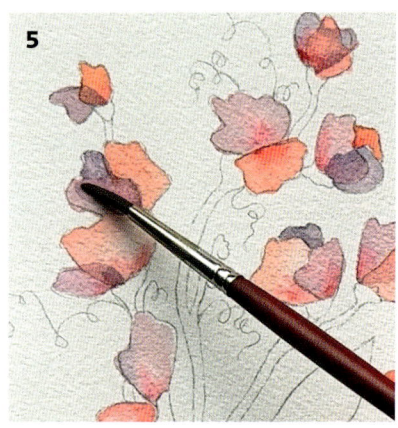
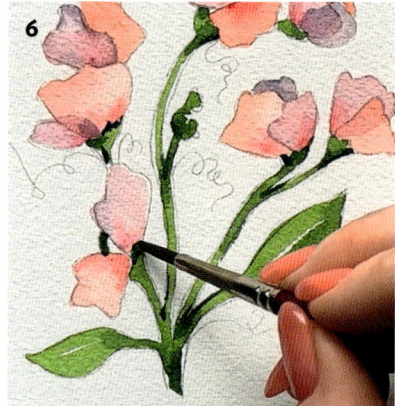
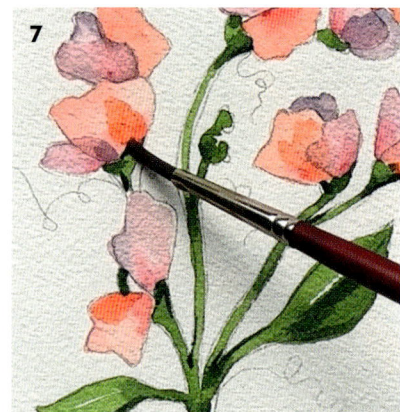
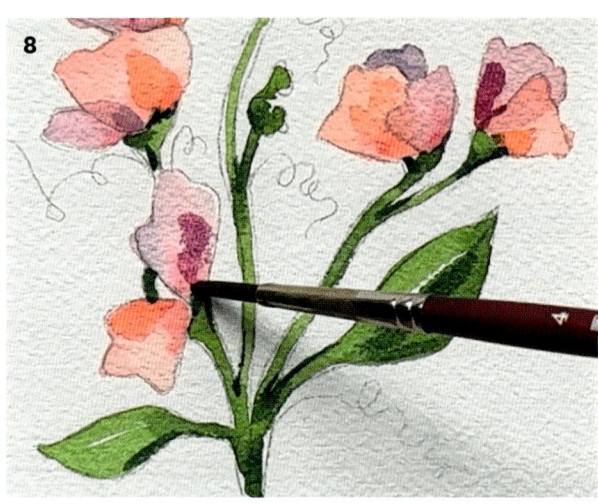
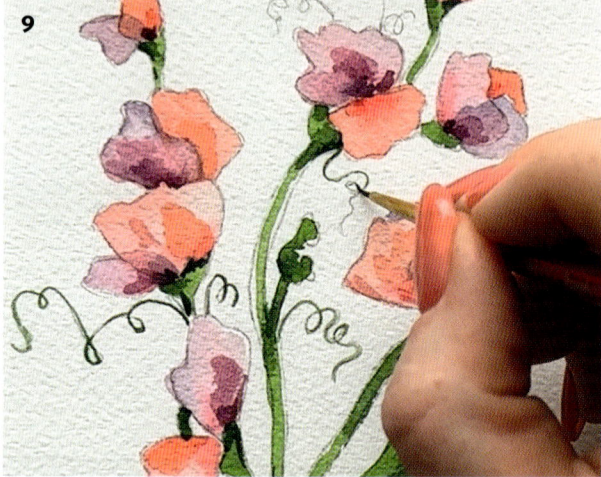

5 Layering: Use the previous pink and purple mixtures to add layered, overlapping washes once the petals are dry.

6 Greenery: Mix lemon yellow, sap green, and a bit of ultramarine to create a light bright green and apply this color to all the greenery and leaves. Add more ultramarine to the mixture of green on your palette to create a deep green for shadows. Add this color around the stems, where the flowers meet the greenery and on the leaves.

7 Pink glaze: Create a light glaze by mixing the previous pink mixture from step 1 with water and adding that color to the pink petals now that they are completely dry. The added glazes can stay as hard lines, or you can rinse your brush and with a damp watery brush, blend the color out into smoother lines within the petal.

8 Purple glaze: Create a glaze for the purple petals using the purple mixture from step 3 and adding water for transparency. Add this color to the purple petals now that they are completely dry.

9 Tendrils: Mix lemon yellow, sap green, and ultramarine to create a dark green for the tendrils. Use a super-small detail brush that holds very little pigment and water to keep these details fine.

LILY OF THE VALLEY

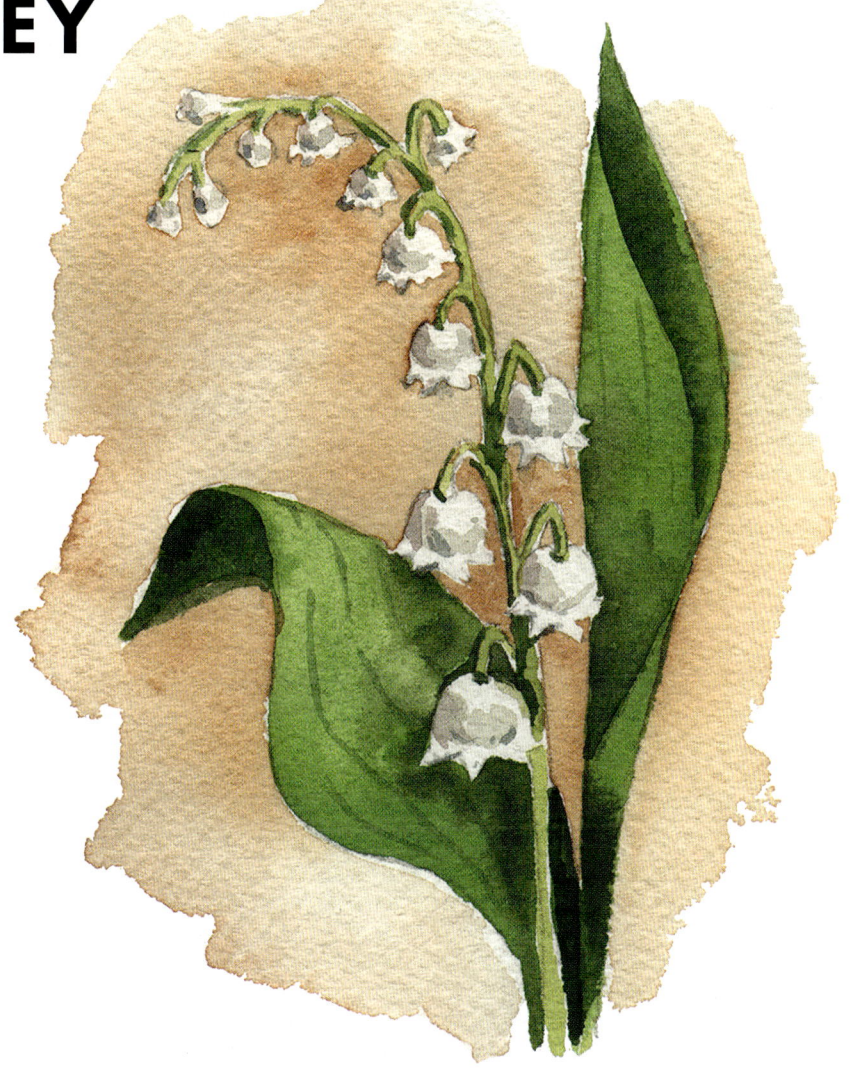

 Cadmium-free yellow

 Ultramarine

 Cadmium-free red

 Sap green

 Lemon yellow

 Burnt sienna

 *Scan the QR code to paint along.*

1 **Leaves:** Mix cadmium-free yellow and sap green to get a bright warm green for the base color. Paint both leaves in a medium wash, being careful to go around the flowers that are white. If the colors feel too dark, you can lift some areas out using a clean, damp brush. Add ultramarine to the green mixture on your palette. This creates a deep green color perfect for shadows. Tap it into the base green color while it's still wet around the flowers and where the natural shadows would be.

2 **Stem:** Mix lemon yellow and cerulean to get a bright light green color for the stem. This color should stand out against the leaves. Add this color to the main stem and all the smaller stems as they connect to the flowers.

3 **Flower "white" base:** You need to use color to paint the flowers "white," but in this project you are also painting a colorful background to help them stand out, so you don't need to fill in the whole flower with color. Use a light wash of ultramarine and cadmium-free red to make a light gray and focus the color only on the left side and around the bottom of the bell without going to the pointed ends.

4 **Flower shadows:** Mix a slightly more pigmented wash of ultramarine and cadmium-free red and focus the deeper shadow on one side. Stay consistent with your shadow color for all the flowers.

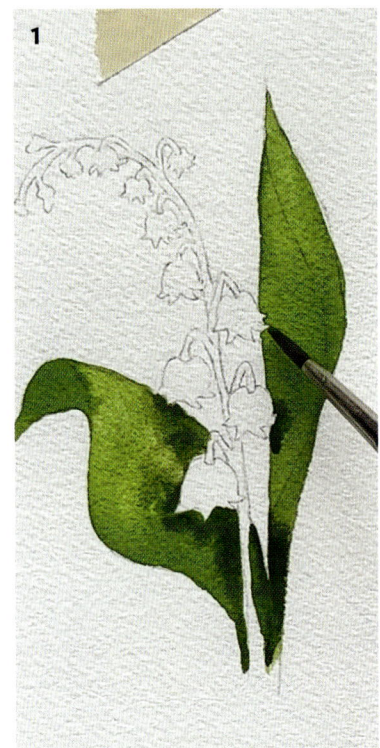
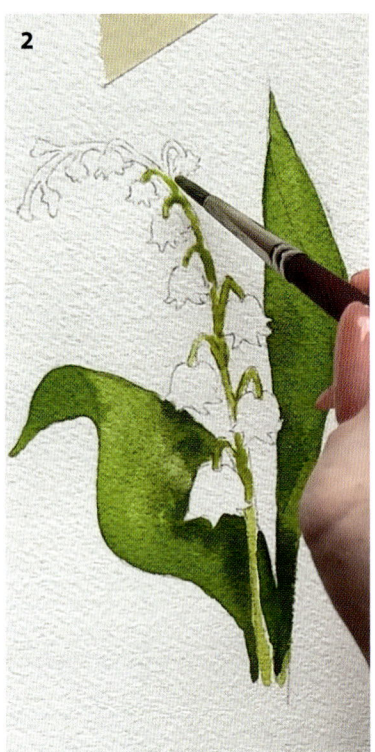
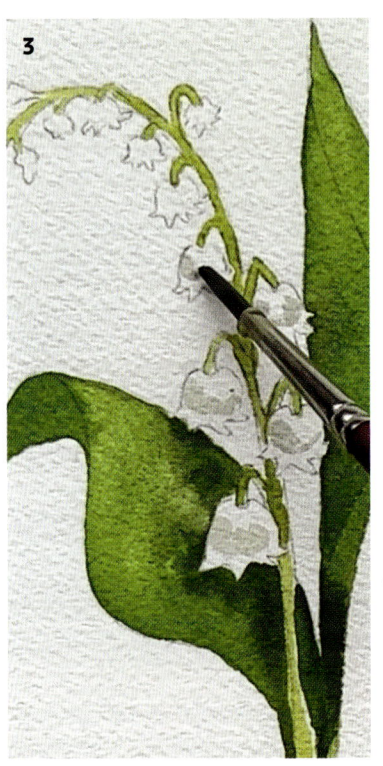
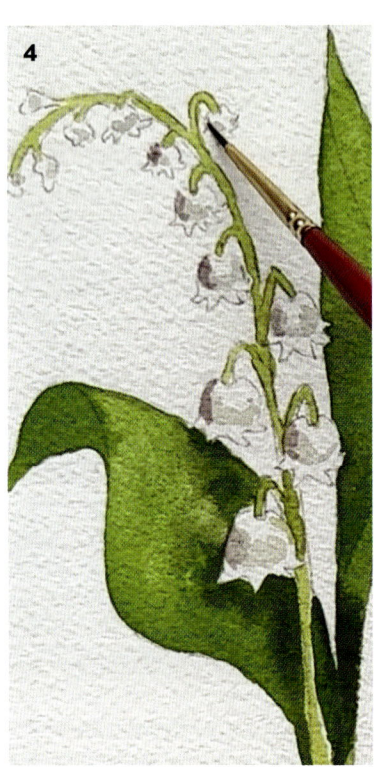

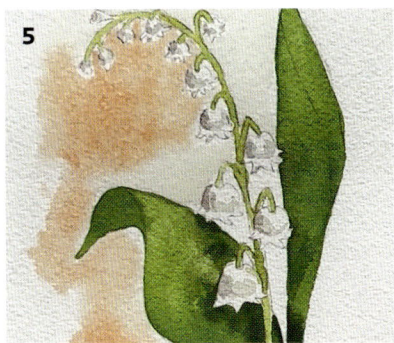
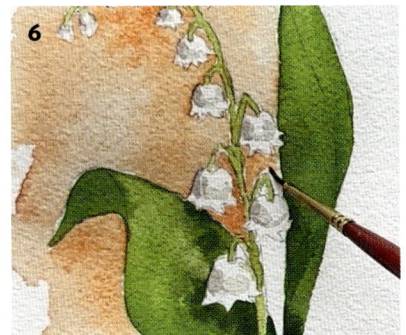
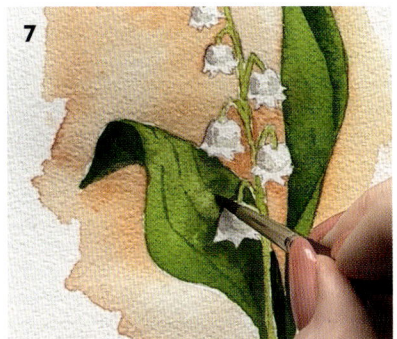
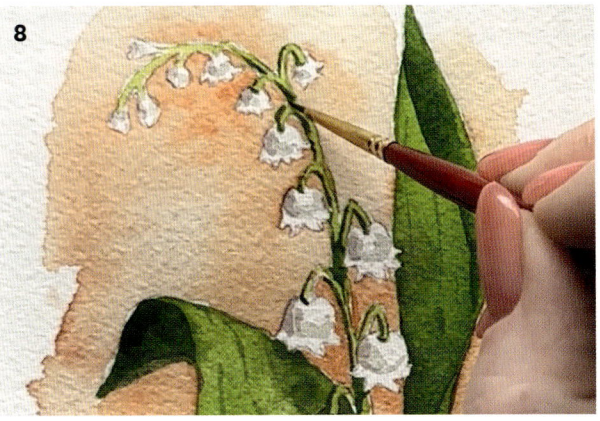
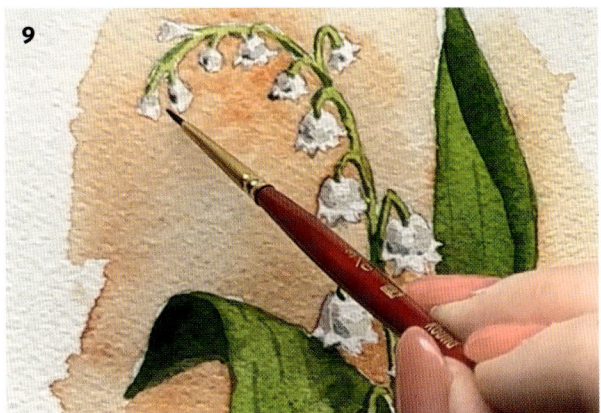

5 **Background:** Now we will add the background by first starting with clean water. Paint carefully with clean water all around the flowers and the leaves. This helps the color disperse evenly so you don't get any hard lines. Next, tap a wash of burnt sienna into the wet areas around the flowers and leaves. This will help the white of the flowers stand out. Move quickly so the paper doesn't dry and you can float the color between all the details of the flowers.

6 **Background intensity:** Add more burnt sienna while the paper is still wet to get a deeper color and use a smaller brush for the details around the flowers. You can work the background in sections to keep the paper wet, and I thought it was fun to keep the edge raw and textured.

7 **Greenery shadows and veins:** Mix ultramarine and sap green to create a deep green for the shadows in the greenery. Add this color under the twist to the left so that the leaf looks like it's flopping over, to the inside of the wrapped leaf, and to the base of the leaves where there would be a natural shadow. Using that same deep green, add a few line details for the veins in the leaves, making sure to curve and taper them with the shape of the leaf.

8 **Stem details:** Add more ultramarine to your green mixture to deepen the color. Use a small detail brush to add shadows on the left side of the main stem and the smaller stems where they connect to the flowers.

9 **Deeper flower shadows:** Add a light wash of ultramarine to the shadow side of the flowers. Make sure you curve the strokes to give the impression of the curved bell shape of the flower.

HAWTHORN

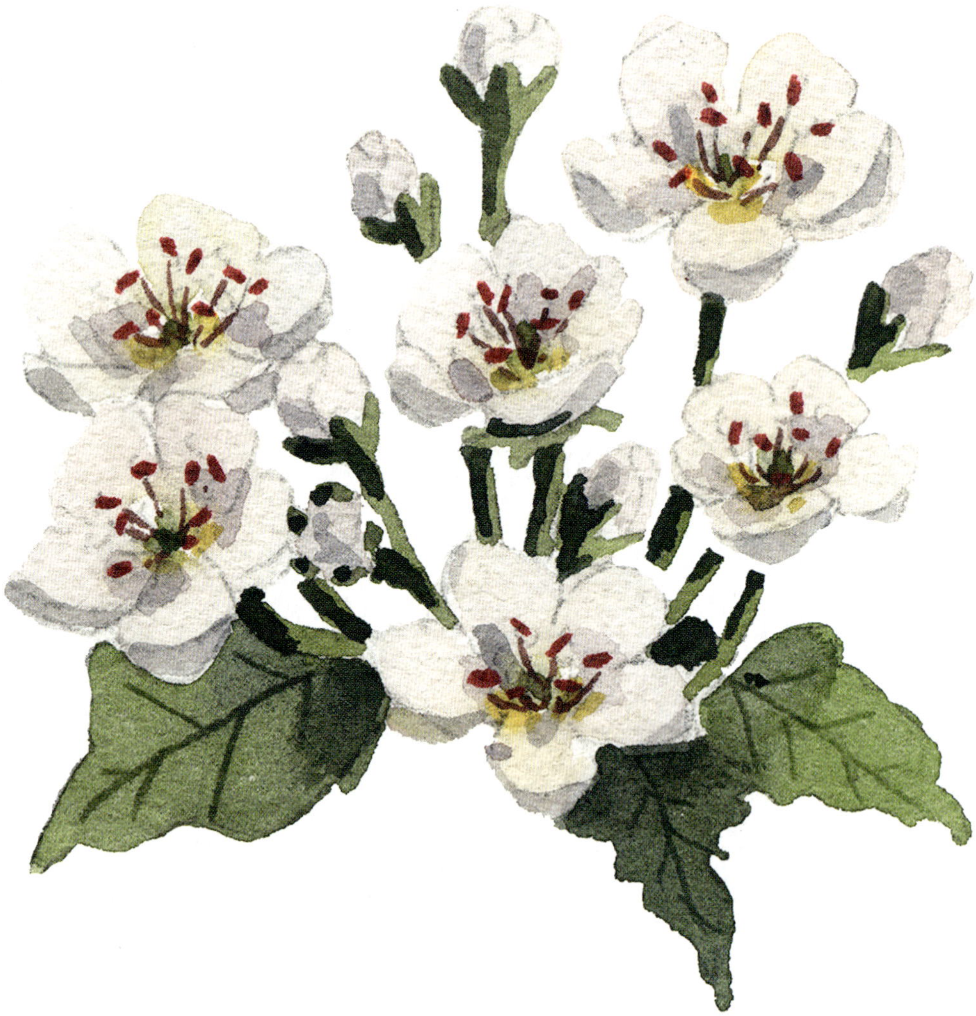

 Cerulean

 Ultramarine

 Sap green

 Lemon yellow

 Cadmium-free red

 Permanent rose

 Cadmium-free yellow

 Burnt sienna

Scan the QR code to paint along.

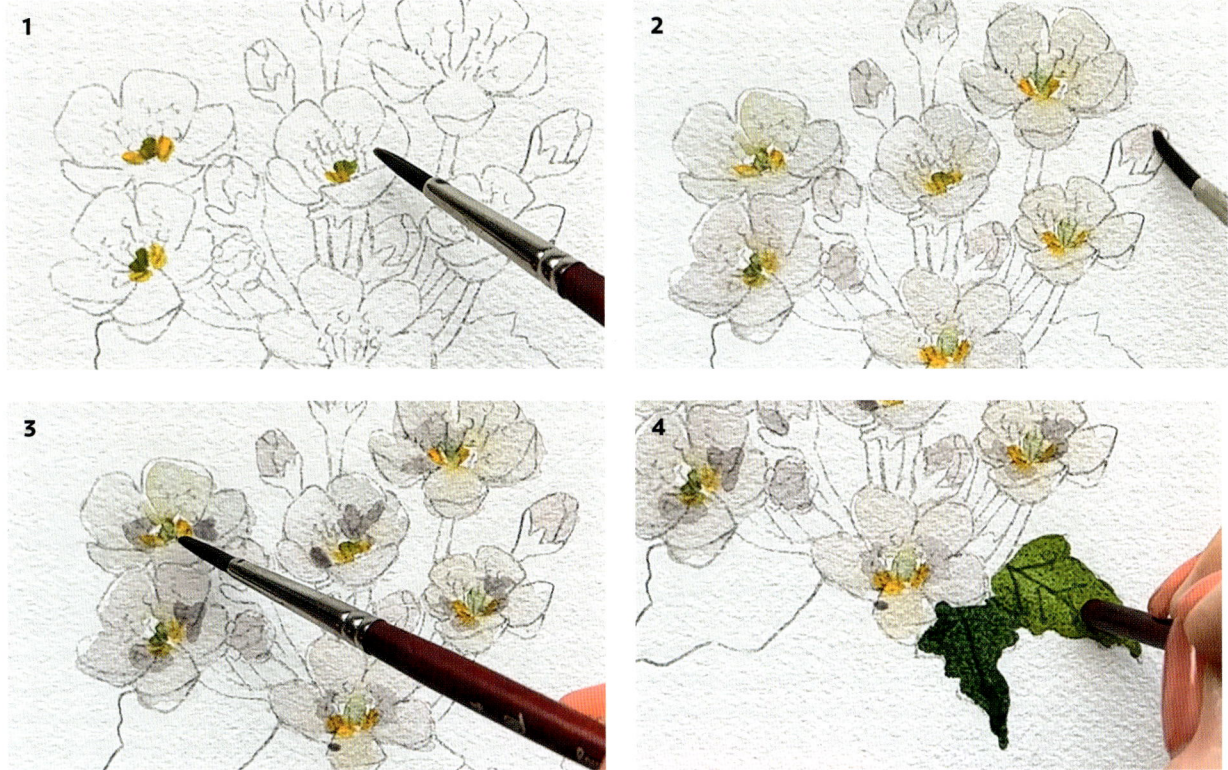

1 **Flower centers:** Mix cerulean and lemon yellow to create a bright green color and add a small dot of this wash to the center of the flowers. Add a medium wash of cadmium-free yellow to each side of the green at the center of each flower. Move on to the next step quickly.

2 **Petal "white" base:** Mix ultramarine, cadmium-free red, and burnt sienna with a lot of water to get a very light value. Tap this color into the center colors slightly and use the shape of the brush to pull the color out, creating light rounded petals. I like to do all of these steps in sections, making sure the center color is still slightly wet when I do the petals and then move onto another section. Repeat for all flowers. For the buds, just focus on the blue gray petal color since the center is not visible.

3 **Petal shadows:** Add more ultramarine to the mixture on your palette to get a deeper shadow color. Paint this darker color around the centers of the flowers in small sections. Less is more with this, because you still want the petals to look white.

4 **Leaves and veins:** For the base green color, mix cadmium-free yellow, sap green, and a touch of ultramarine to get a light yellow-green. Create bumpy leafy textures that start wide at the flowers and come to a point. Add more ultramarine to your green mixture and paint another leaf that touches to create a light bleed of greens while everything is still wet. While the leaves are still wet, flip your brush around to the hard end and gently push into the paper, creating a veined pattern. This works because the indentation allows paint to flow in, creating a slightly darker line.

5 Repeat the previous steps on all leaves and fill in all the stems and sepals connecting the flowers to the greenery with the light base green color.

6 **Filaments:** Pick up a concentrated amount of permanent rose for the filaments at the end of the stamen. Dot them in unevenly, creating small rectangular shapes around the center of the flower.

7 **Stem shadows:** Mix more sap green and ultramarine into your green mixture to get a deeper green shadow color. Add this color to one side of all your stems consistently to represent shadow.

8 **Stamens:** Add some of your green wash to your permanent rose mixture to get a slightly deeper pigment for the stamen lines of the flower. These are the lines that connect the filaments to the center of the flower. Make sure they are uneven and slightly curved to show movement.

9 **Deeper petal shadows:** Add a final bit of shadow to the flower petals. Mix ultramarine into your deep red stamen mixture with water to get a lighter wash, focusing some of the color on the outside of the petals in the more shadowy areas underneath where the petals curve up.

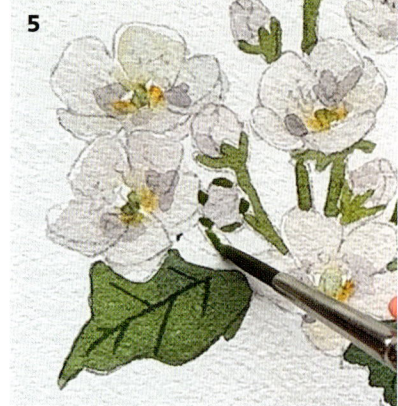
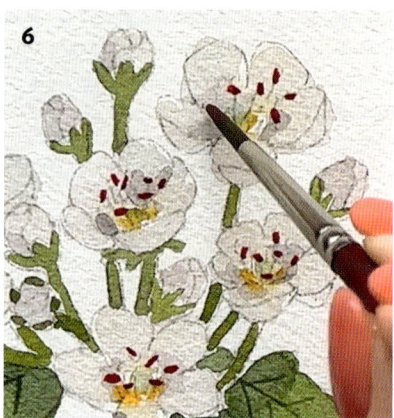
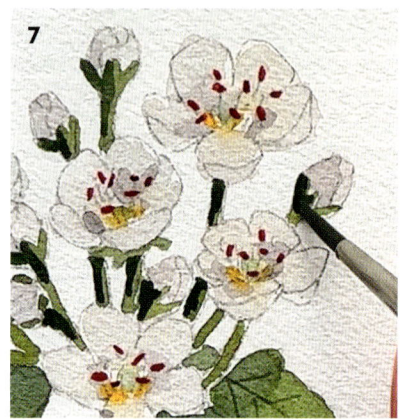
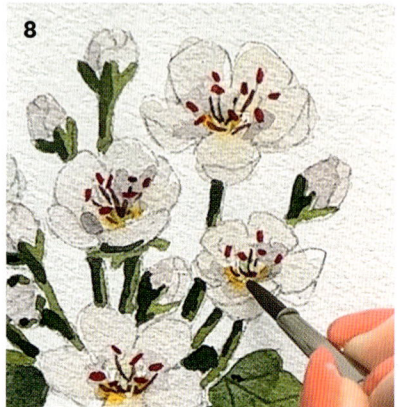
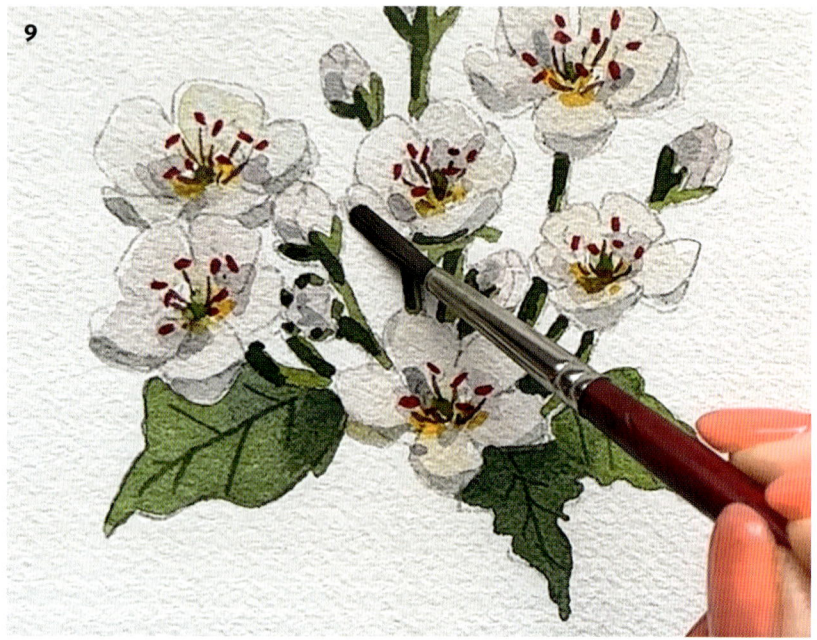

HONEYSUCKLE

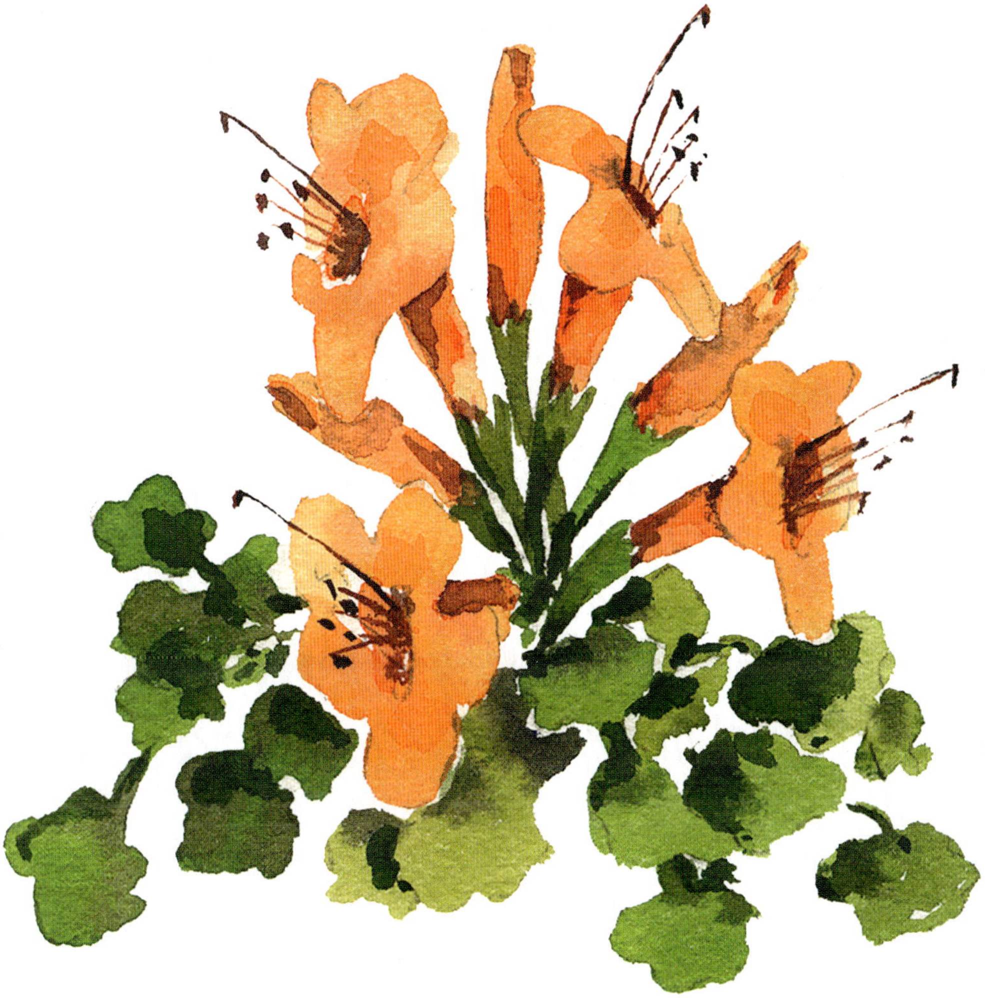

 Cadmium-free red

 Cadmium-free yellow

 Sap green

 Ultramarine

 Permanent rose

 *Scan the QR code to paint along.*

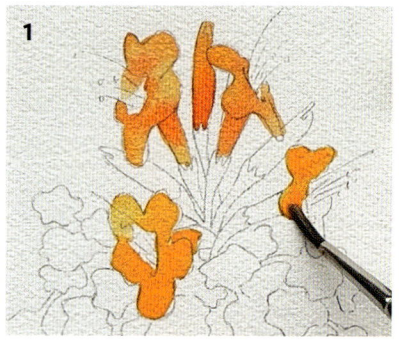
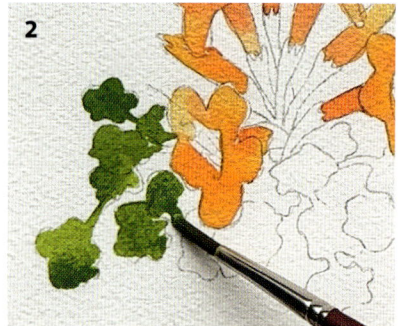
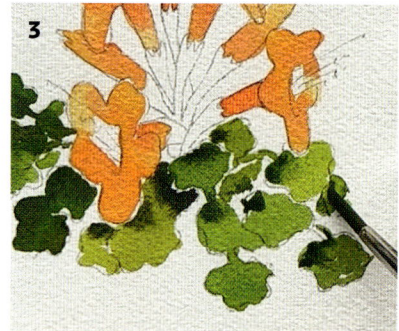
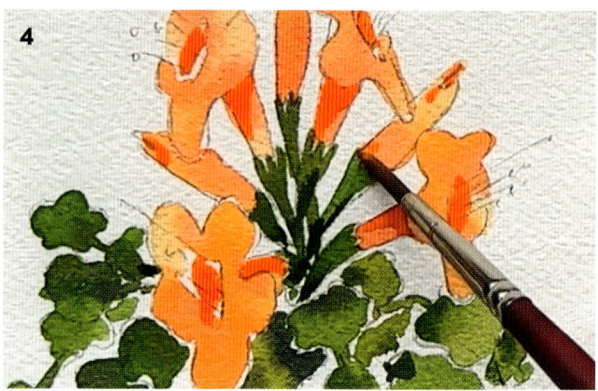
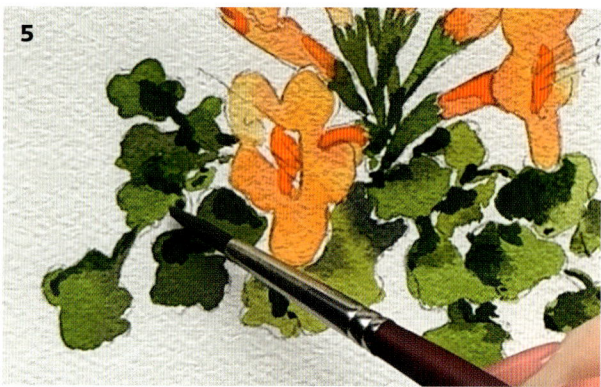

1 **Petal base color:** Mix cadmium-free red and cadmium-free yellow to create a light orange wash and paint the flowers leaving the centers open. Think of the honeysuckle shape as a top crown and a bottom crown with a trumpet shape connecting the flower to the stem. Paint all flowers with light orange wash including the buds. You can add different variations of the colors (magenta, red, yellow, orange) while you paint so that there is dimension within each flower.

2 **Greenery base color:** Mix sap green and cadmium-free yellow to create a medium wash and add that color in circular strokes to make circular, textured leafy bunches. Move quickly to the next step before the green dries.

3 **Greenery shadows:** Add ultramarine to the green mixture on the palette to create a deep green. Tap this color into the base green color while it's still wet to get a gradual shadowy blend. Focus the color where the leaves meet the stems and where a natural shadow would be. Bring the light green up onto the stems, connecting the leaves to the flowers, and add the darker green in a few places while it's still wet.

4 **Petal shadows:** Mix cadmium-free red and cadmium-free yellow to create a deep orange color. Add this to the centers of the flowers and just under the top petals on the trumpet part. Also add a few strokes on the buds.

5 **Deeper greenery shadows:** Once the leaves are completely dry, mix sap green and ultramarine to get a dark green for contrast. The lines will be hard, but you can use water to smooth some of them out. Keep this deep contrasting color to a minimum so you don't overpower the medium values.

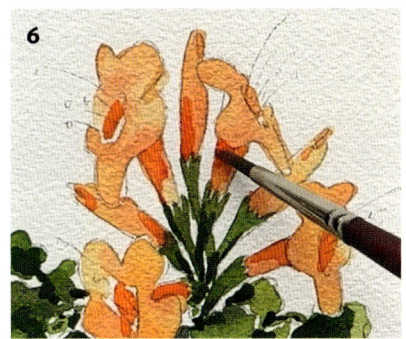

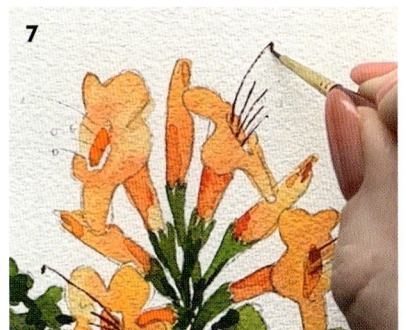

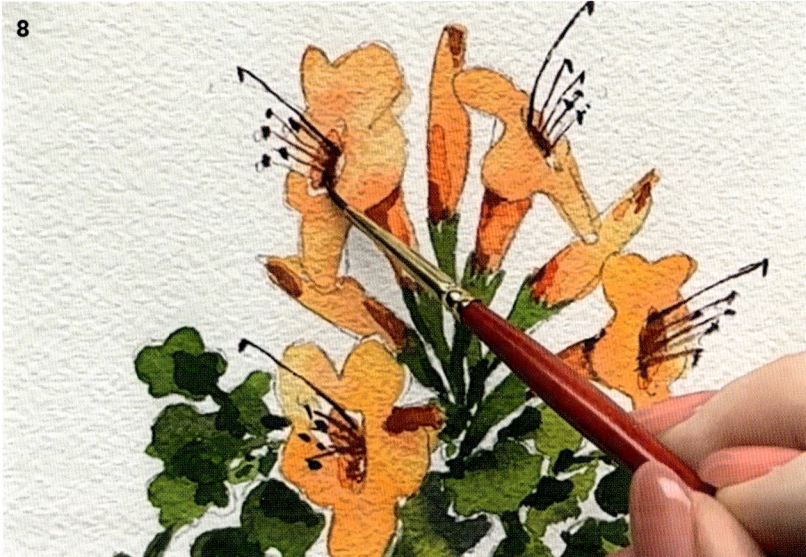

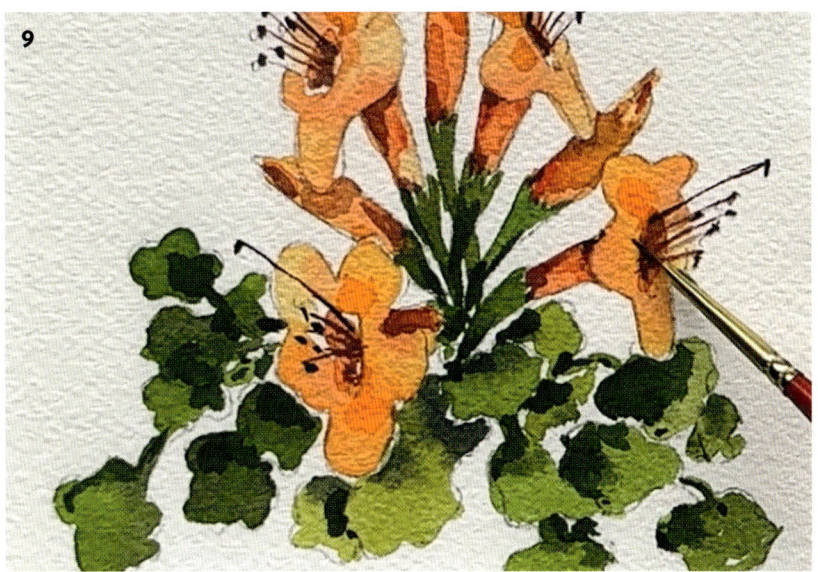

6 **Petal shadows:** Add more cadmium-free red to the orange mix on your palette to create a glaze and paint this color on some areas of the flowers to create more dimension. In places where the lines are too hard or there is too much pigment, you can blend out the colors with a damp brush.

7 **Stamens:** Mix ultramarine, permanent rose, and cadmium-free red to create a deep magenta color for the stamen at the center of the honeysuckle. There is a top stamen that is very long and then three or four shorter stamens in the middle. Add more ultramarine to the mix and paint tiny rectangles at the end of each stamen for the filaments.

8 **Deeper petal shadows:** Apply the stamen color on the trumpet part of the flowers just under the top petals. Use a minimal amount so that light, medium, and dark values are all visible. Also lightly add this color to the centers to give the impression that the flower is a cone and goes deeper.

9 **Final glaze:** Use the orange washes on your palette to create a glaze, and a light wash of this color in areas around the buds and petals to give them more dimension.

JUNE

ROSE

 Permanent rose

 Cadmium-free yellow

 Ultramarine

 Sap green

 *Scan the QR code to paint along.*

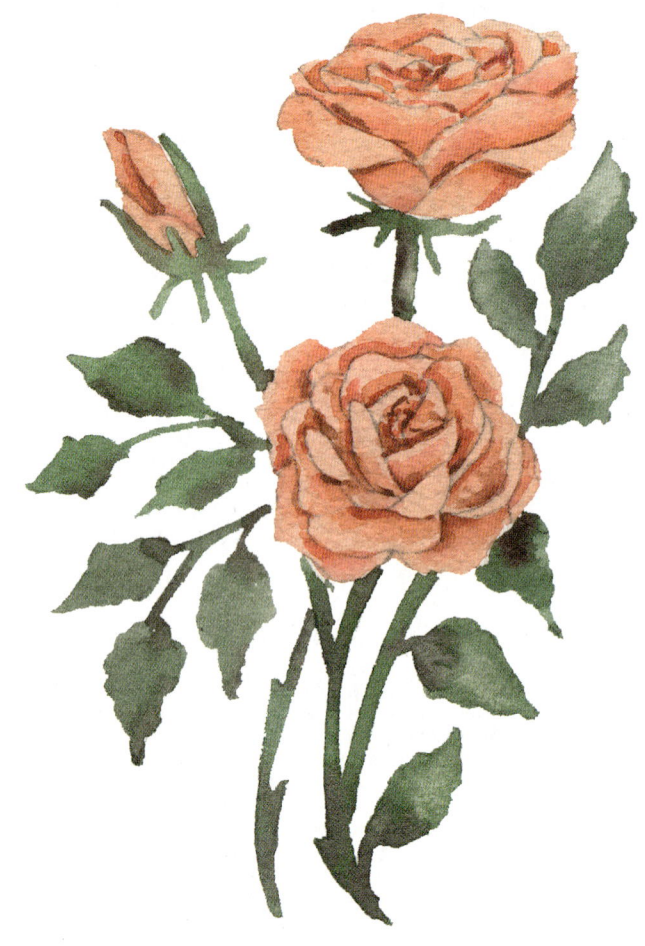

1 **Petal base color:** Mix permanent rose and cadmium-free yellow to create a light wash for the base of the rose. Fill in both flowers and the bud with the mixture.

2 **Greenery base color:** Mix ultramarine and sap green and add it to the stems and leaves in sections so that they stay wet. Then add more ultramarine with a touch of permanent rose to the green mixture to create a deep green color for the shadows. Tap this color in while the base color

is still wet to get natural blending shadows. Focus the shadow color at the base of the leaves and under the flowers, where deeper colors would be found in real life.

3 **Lifting color:** If you have good medium and dark values but have lost the lighter areas, rinse your brush, tap it on your paper towel, and use the damp brush to lift out paint while everything is still wet. This looks great on the tip of the leaves so that the deeper values naturally fade into the stems.

4 **Petal shadows:** Mix cadmium-free yellow and permanent rose to create a deeper pink color and use it to start building up depth within the petals. Think of a flower like a cone. The petals fan outward, forming the outer ring of the cone, but they all taper together at a point until they attach at the stem. The place where they start bunching together and attaching at the stem is where you want to build up these deeper colors. Leave the tips of the petals the lighter pink where they catch the

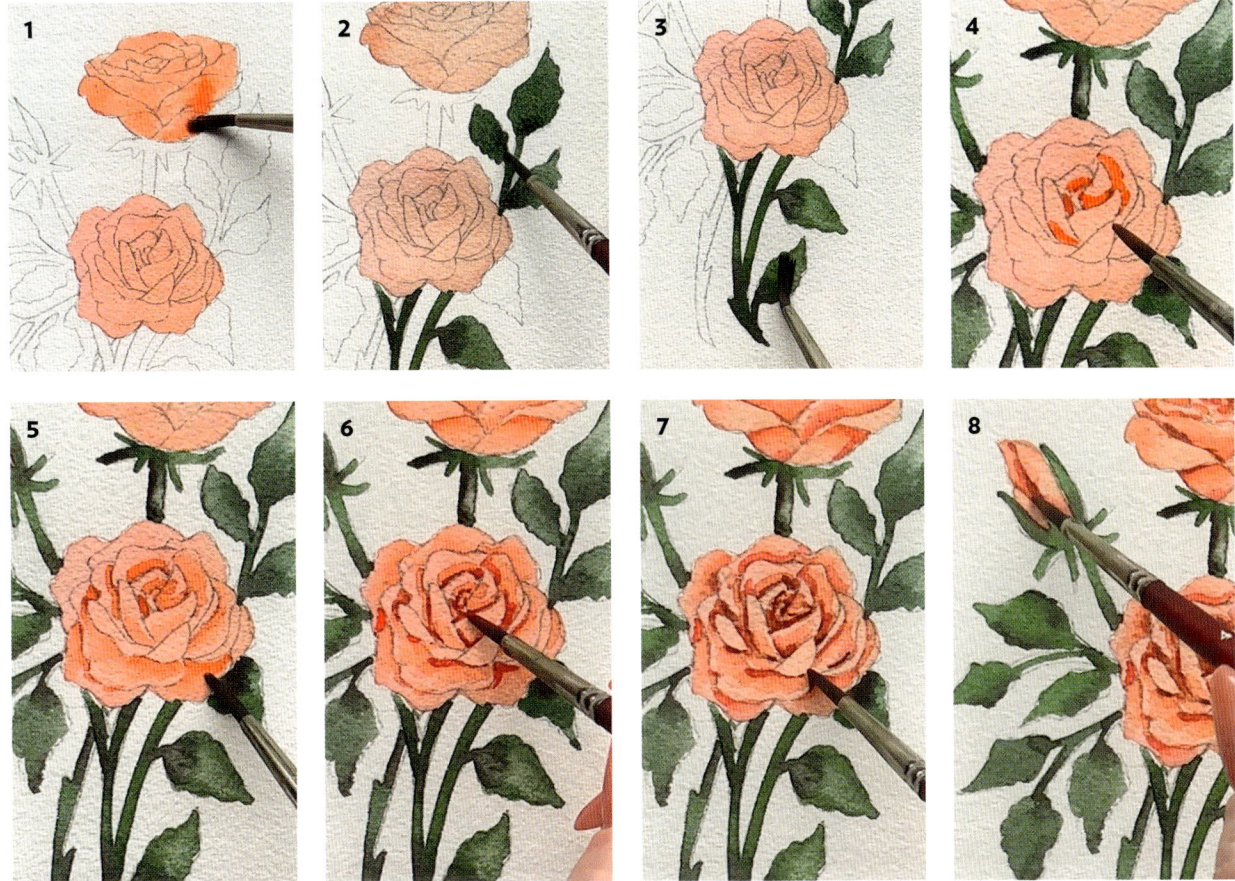

light. Remember that differently positioned petals will have different shadows.

5 **Blending:** Once you add the deeper color in a few spots, rinse your brush, blot it on a paper towel, and use the damp brush to smooth out the color. You want the color to fade lightly into the light tips of the petals without painting the tips.

6 **Deeper petal shadows:** Add more permanent rose to your pink mixture to create a deeper color and continue to build up the layers of shadow. Try not to overtake the medium values you just placed and use a minimal amount of this color. This darker color can be left as a hard line or you can blend it out like before using a damp brush. You might want to have a little bit of both for a loose-detailed style.

7 **Darkest petal shadows:** In some areas on the flower the shadows can be even deeper because the petals are so tightly pushed together, and less light gets in. This is mostly toward the center of each rose. Add ultramarine to your cadmium-free yellow and permanent rose mixture to deepen the color and add a few areas of the darkest shadows.

8 **Bud details:** Add the layers of shadows to create depth just at the line where the petals start to open.

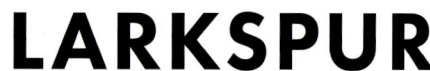

LARKSPUR

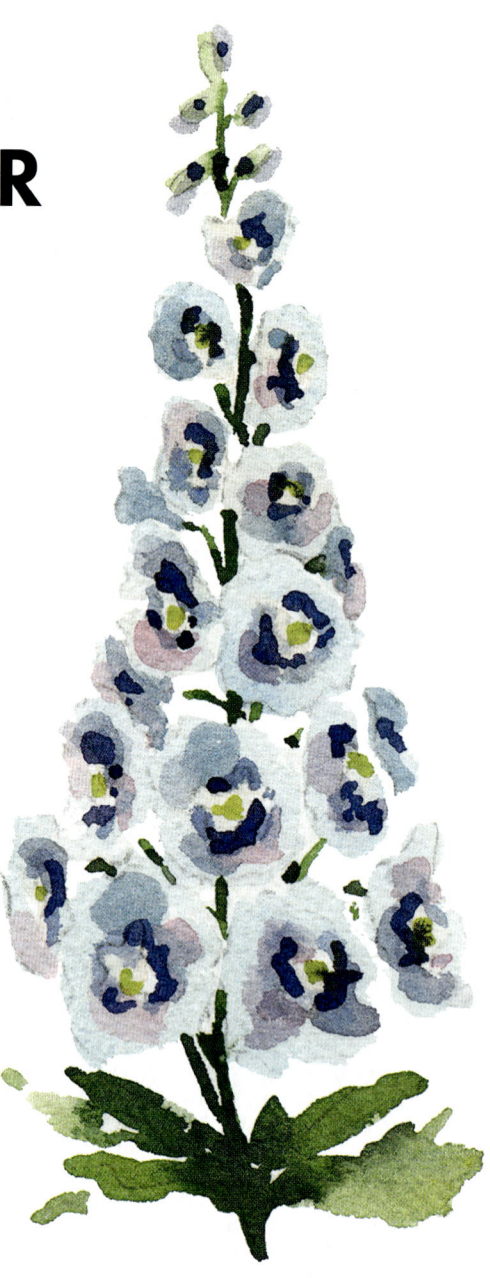

 Burnt sienna

 Ultramarine

 Cerulean

 Sap green

 Cadmium-free yellow

 Permanent rose

 Lemon yellow

 Cadmium-free red

 *Scan the QR code to paint along.*

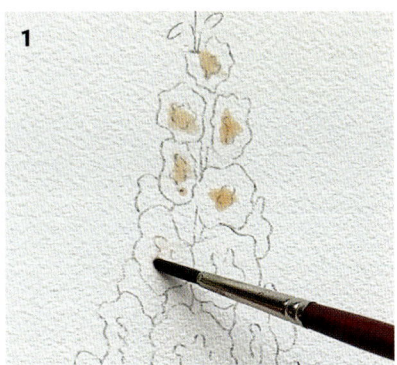
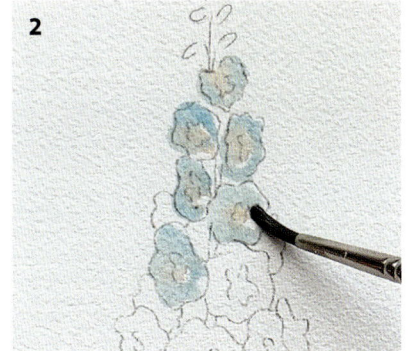
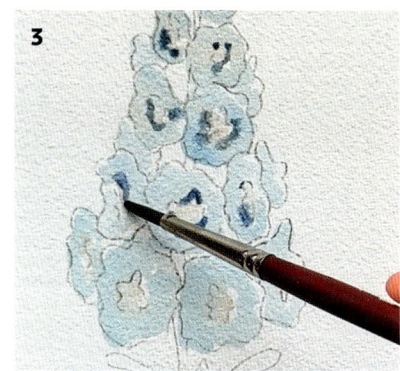
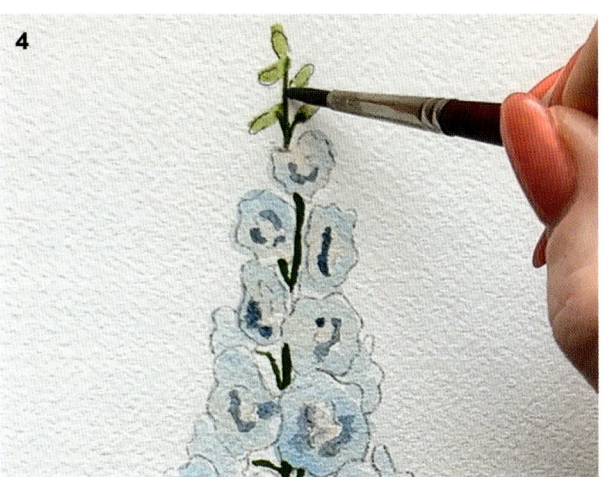
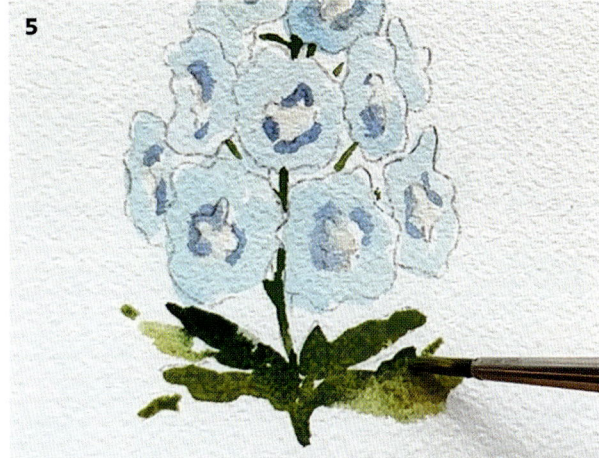

1 Flower centers: Mix burnt sienna with a touch of ultramarine to create a light creamy tan color. Paint this loosely in the center section of the flowers. Move on to the next step quickly.

2 Petal base color: Pick up a light wash of cerulean. While the centers are still wet, loosely paint this wash in a circular scribbling motion around the centers, leaving some areas of white space.

3 Petal shadows: Pick up a deeper wash of ultramarine and paint this color around the centers to help define them. Sometimes it's nice when the flowers are still a little bit wet so you get a nice bleed, but hard lines are great here too. Don't connect them all the way; just a few lines will do the trick.

4 Stalk and buds: Mix sap green, cadmium-free yellow, and ultramarine to get a base green color for the greenery. This is a darker green color because it is more in shadow as it's tucked in under the flowers. Paint the stalk and the little stems coming off it that are attached to the flowers. Mix cadmium-free yellow into the green mixture to get a brighter yellow green color. Tap it into some bud shapes at the top of the painting while the stalk is still wet so that they naturally blend.

5 Greenery: Use both green colors mixed in step 4 to paint leaves. Use rough shapes tapered to a point at the end, letting them bleed together to get dimension.

6   **Deeper petal shadows:** Mix up a light wash of cerulean and ultramarine with a touch of permanent rose and start building up the blue values and dimension within the flower petals. Add this color in some of the curvier areas of the petals, but be careful not to overpower the lighter values.

7   **Glaze petals with lavender:** When the paper is dry, add more permanent rose to the purple mix from step 6 to get a light lavender wash. Use it to glaze over some of the flower petals and create layers within the blue tones. Mix in a little bit of ultramarine to this light purple color and create very tiny strokes where the buds are to create the impression that there are little flowers coming out and getting ready to bloom.

8   **Center details:** Mix lemon yellow into the green on your palette for a bright yellow green color and dot it in each of the centers of the flowers, making sure not to fill the entire space but leave room around it.

9   **Final glaze:** Once everything has completely dried, mix ultramarine, cadmium-free red, and permanent rose to add a deeper blue around the centers to really help everything pop. This adds contrast and creates that layered feel between the light, medium, and dark values. Place it very minimally around the centers of the flowers, making sure not to connect any of the lines in a perfect circle. Use this deeper blue color to add a tiny bit of shadow with a simple small line at the base of the flower buds near the top.

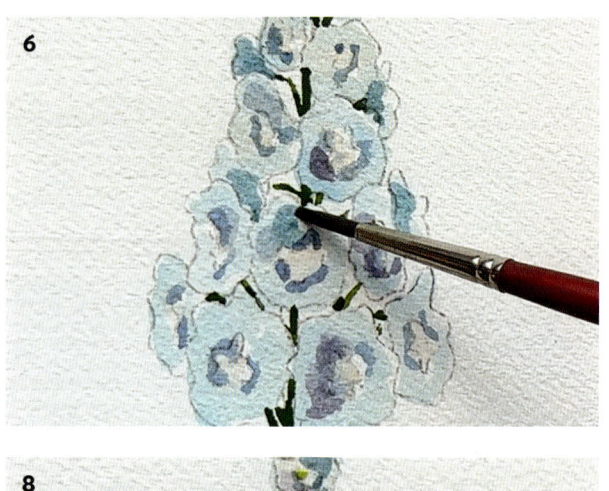

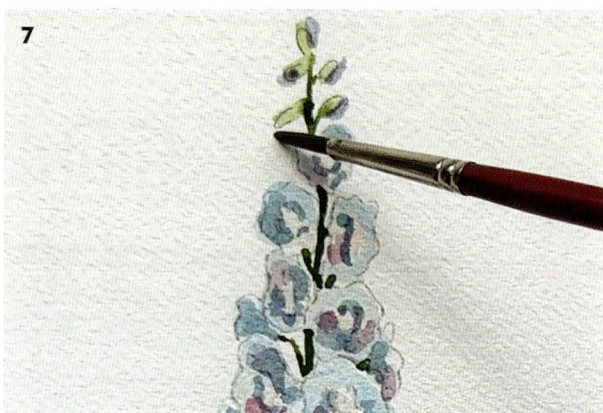

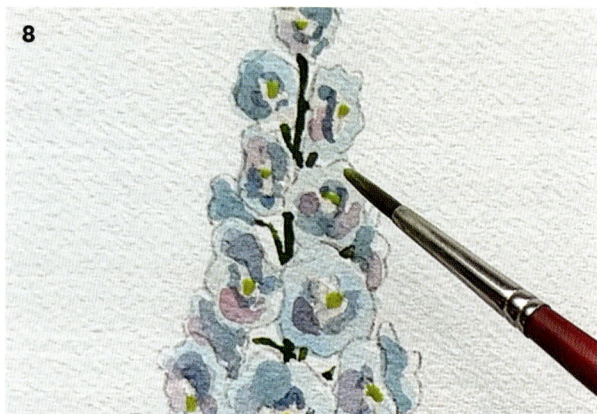

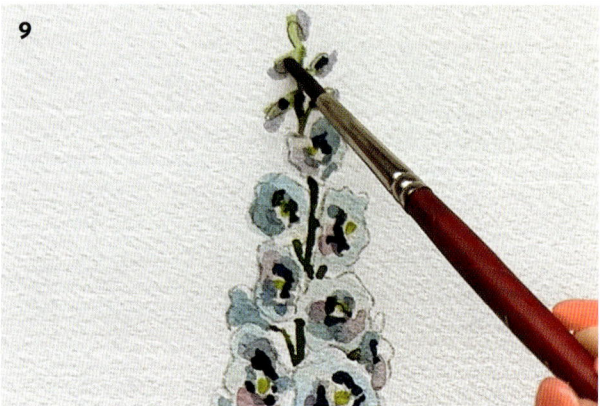

WATER LILY

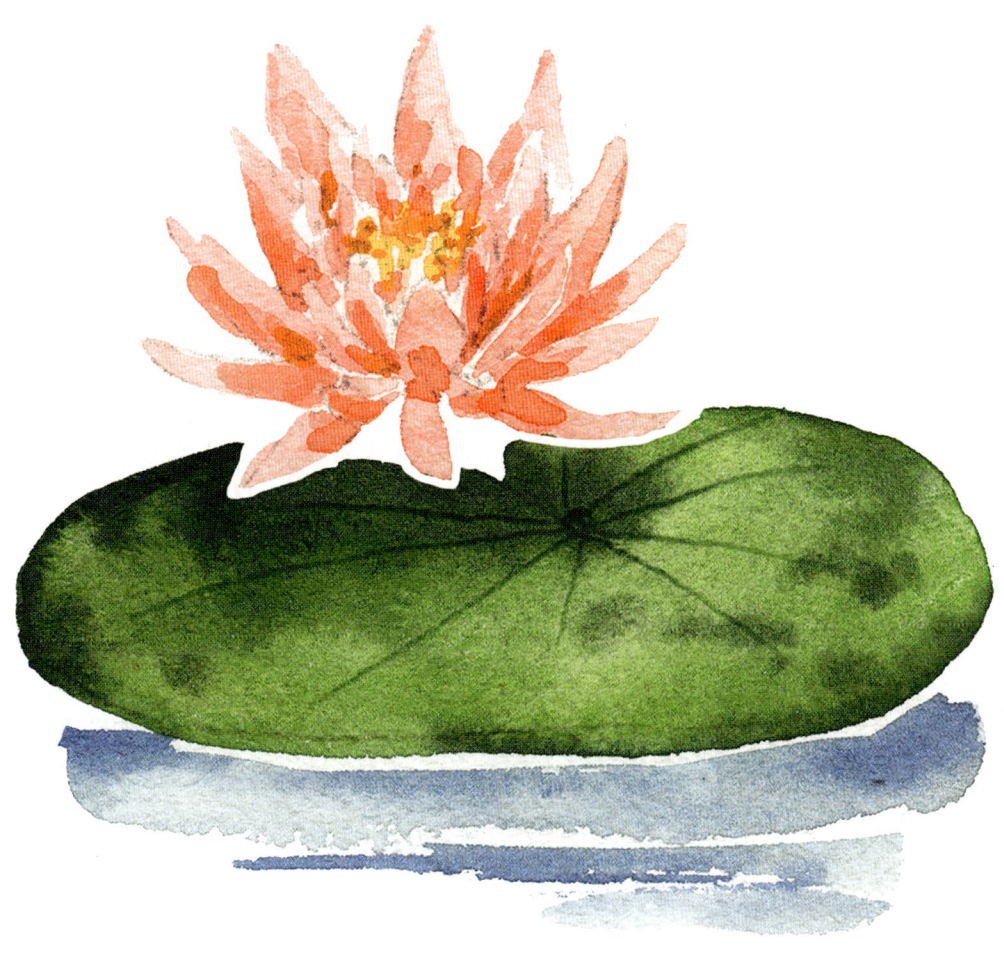

 Cadmium-free yellow

 Sap green

 Cerulean

 Permanent rose

 Ultramarine

 *Scan the QR code to paint along.*

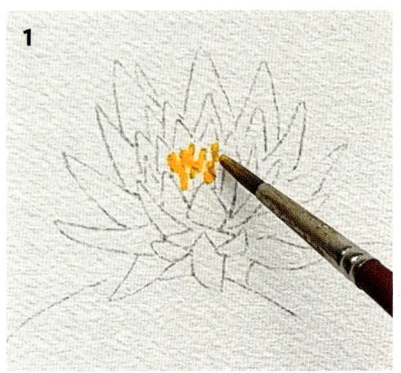
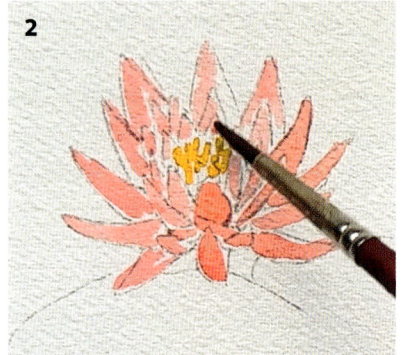
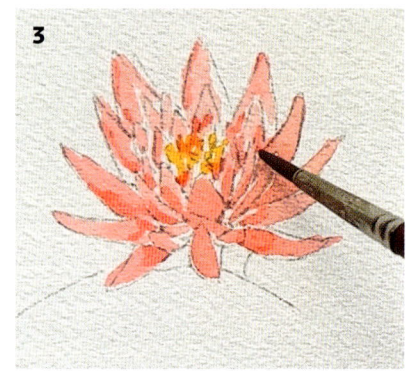
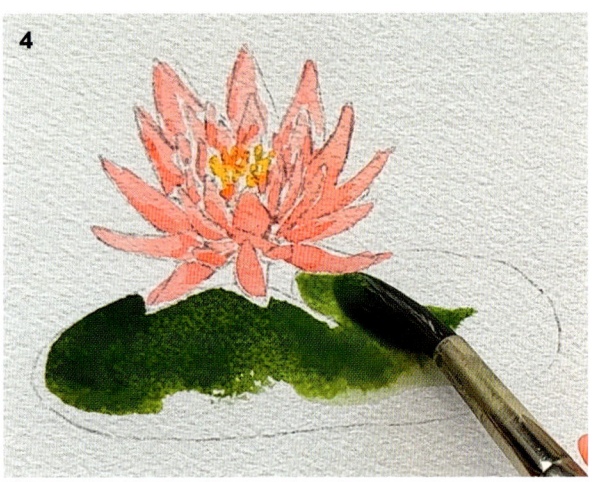
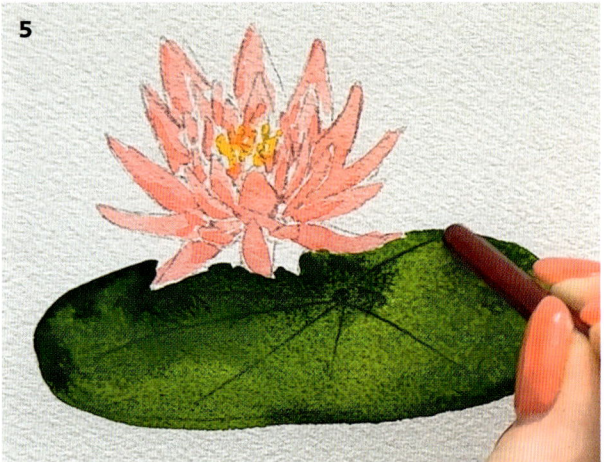

1 **Stamen:** Using a wash of cadmium-free yellow, add small, disconnected strokes at the center of the flower to create the stamen.

2 **Petal base color:** Mix permanent rose with a small amount of cadmium-free yellow to get a bright orangey pink wash. Add this color to the spiky petals of the flower. Make sure to leave some areas of white space so that you can distinguish the petal separation. Bring this light pink wash up and around the back of the flower without touching the center stamen.

3 **Petal shadows:** Add more permanent rose to the orangey pink wash, giving it a darker value. Use it to layer in a deeper pink to create shadows at the base of the petals where they attach to the lily pad.

4 **Lily pad:** Mix sap green, cadmium-free yellow, and ultramarine to get a deep wash of green for the lily pad. Place this color on one edge of the lily pad and use water to help disperse the color so that there is variation between pigmented and watery areas.

5 **Lily pad shadows:** While the lily pad is still wet, add some ultramarine to the green mixture, creating a deep shadow color. Add this color under the water lily and on the edges of the lily pad to give a nice, blended shadow effect. Use the other end of your brush handle to gently push into the paper while the lily pad is still wet to create details and veins in the greenery.

6 **Water:** Add a mixture of cerulean and ultramarine in a light wash at the base of the lily pad to give the impression of water underneath. If you use your brush more parallel to the paper, you can get a nice textured edge with the dry brush technique.

7 **Deeper petal shadows:** When the paper is dry, go in with a darker permanent rose to continue layering the shadows. Focus this color on the very inside of the petals and at the base where they meet the lily pad, keeping the strokes minimal. Some of these pink shadowy areas can have hard lines, but if it is too intense or the line is too hard, rinse your brush, tap the water out on your paper towel, and then with a damp brush, blend the color into the rest of the petal.

8 **Stamen shadows:** Mix cadmium-free yellow with a small amount of permanent rose to get a deep orange. Tap that color where the stamen is to give more fullness and fill in some of that white space you reserved.

9 **Final glaze:** Using the same mixture in step 8, place this wash in a few areas around the petals and in between the stamen for a final shadow.

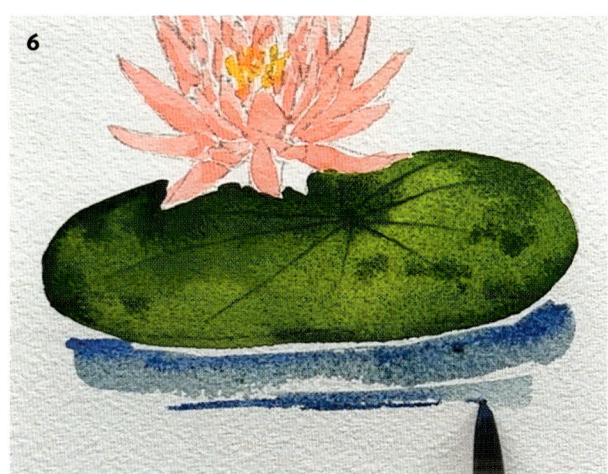

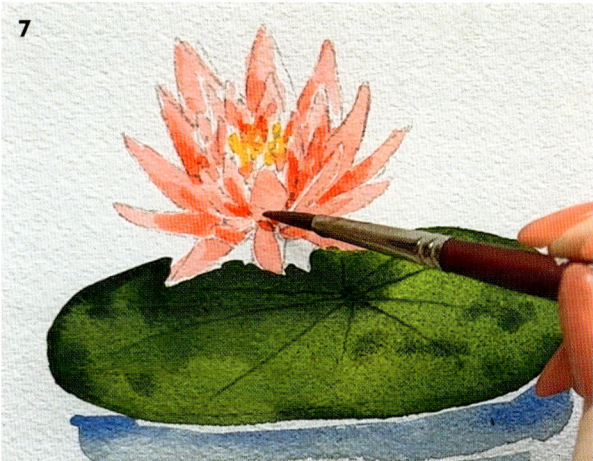

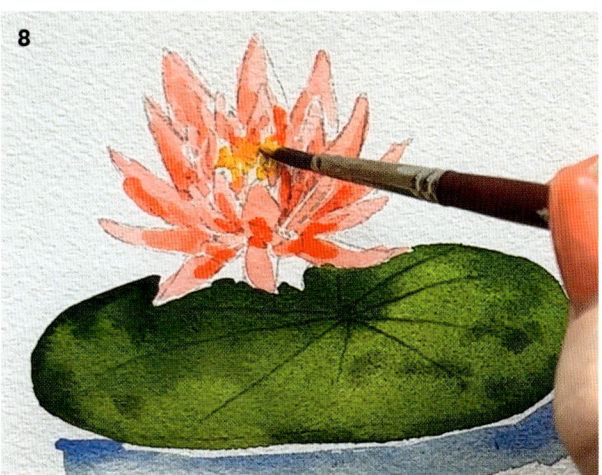

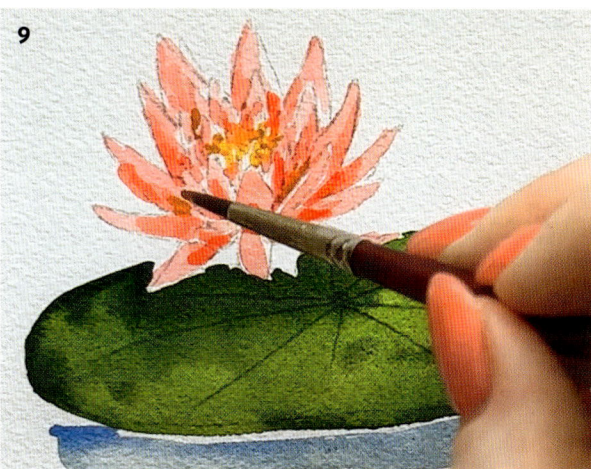

GLADIOLUS

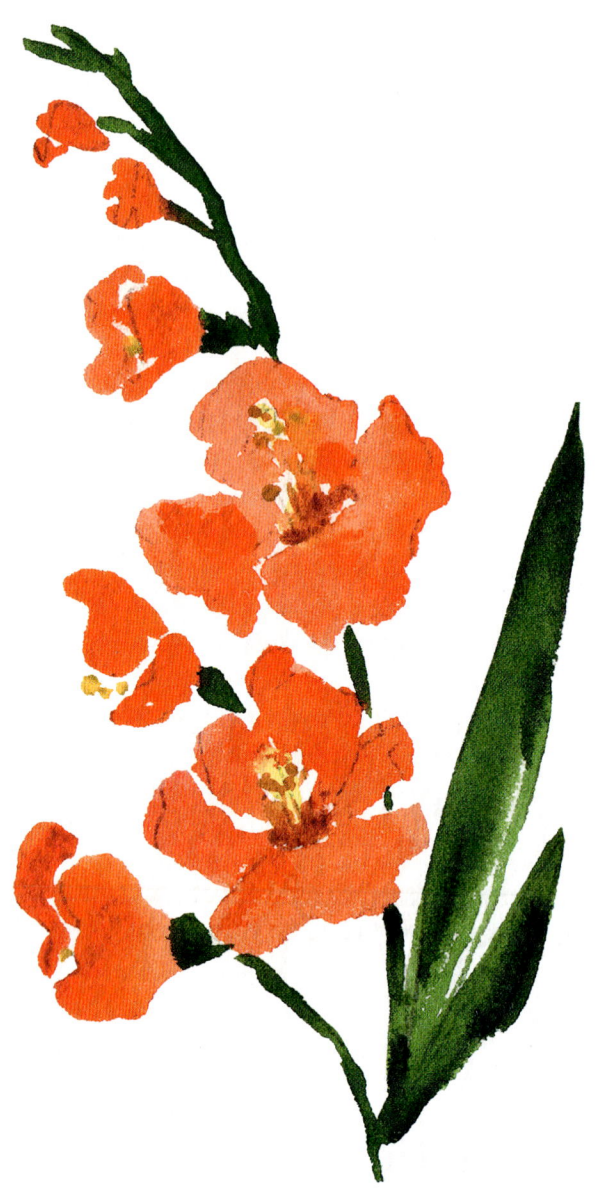

 Lemon yellow

 Permanent Rose

 Sap green

 Cadmium-free red

 Cadmium-free yellow

 Ultramarine

 *Scan the QR code to paint along.*

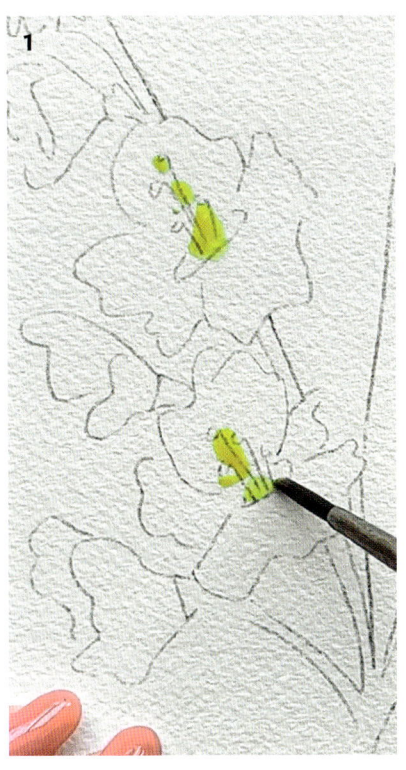

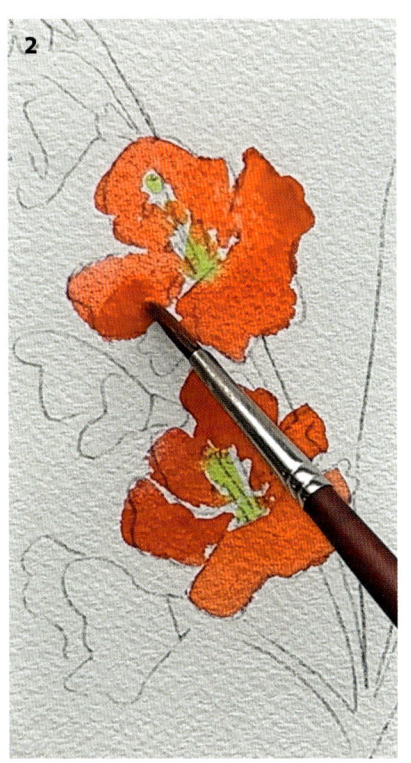

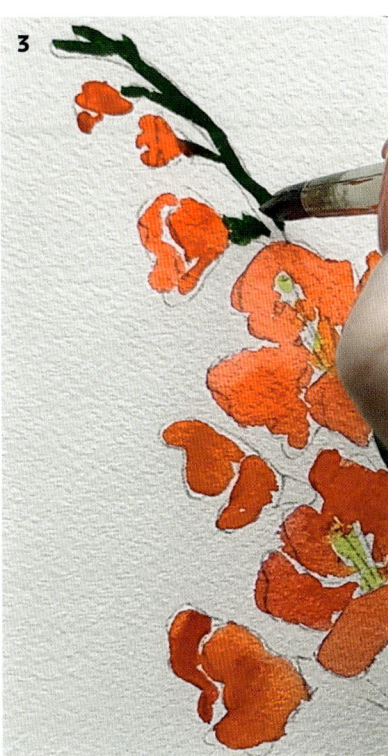

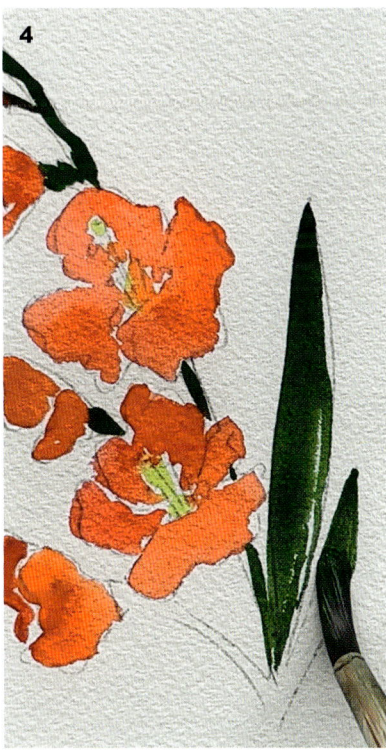

1 **Flower centers:** Pick up a light wash of lemon yellow and add that loosely to the center of each open flower.

2 **Petal base color:** Mix cadmium-free red with a tiny bit of permanent rose to increase the brightness. Use this wash to create fluffy red petals, sweeping around the center of the flower without touching the yellow. Bring the red wash up and around the yellow, going slightly into the center to negatively paint the stamen. Leave a little bit of white space for the separation of the petals. Add the same red magenta wash to the small flower buds, keeping that uneven circular stroke you used for the petals, leaving a gap in between for visual separation.

3 **Stem:** Mix cadmium-free yellow, sap green, and ultramarine to create a deep green color. Start with a thin line for the main stem, then add tiny stems that attach to the buds as you go down.

4 **Leaves:** Paint the leaves starting with the tip of the brush and light pressure, pushing down on the body of the brush to create fullness in the center of the leaf while dragging to connect the leaf to the main stem. Use the same green color as in the previous step.

5 **Leaf shadows:** Add some ultramarine to the green mixture to get a deeper shadowy color of green and tap this into the leaves while everything is still wet.

6 **Stamen shadows:** Mix cadmium-free yellow with a bit of cadmium-free red to get a deep orange color. Use this to add more definition and shadow in the filaments and stamen. Dot this color at the end of the stamen and then make a few lines connecting this color down to the center of the flower.

7 **Petal shadows:** Add permanent rose to a bit of the green mixture to create a deep dark red hue. Place this color at the center of the flower just underneath the stamen to give the flower dimension and depth.

8 **Final glaze:** Add water to the red mixture to use as a glaze. Using the dry brush technique, paint over some of the petals to give more depth and dimension.

9 **Final stamens:** Paint a few dots of cadmium-free yellow at the edges of the buds so that it looks as if the stamen is peeking out of these buds as they are beginning to bloom.

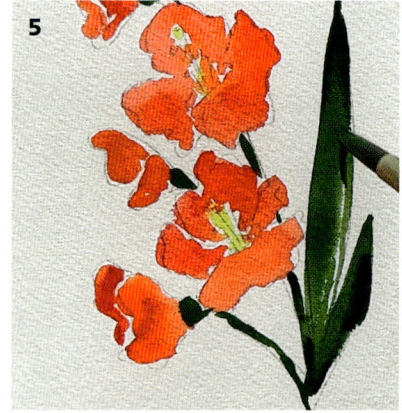
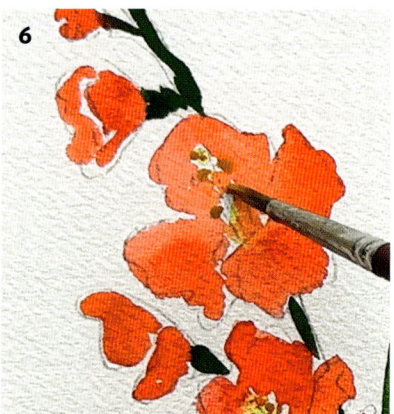
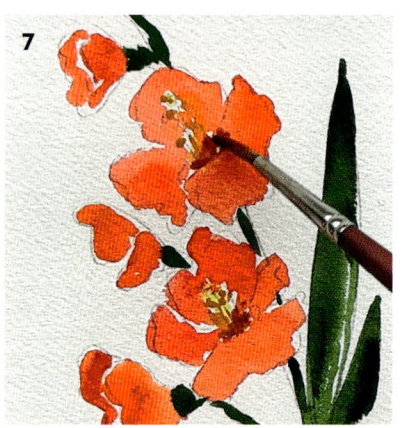
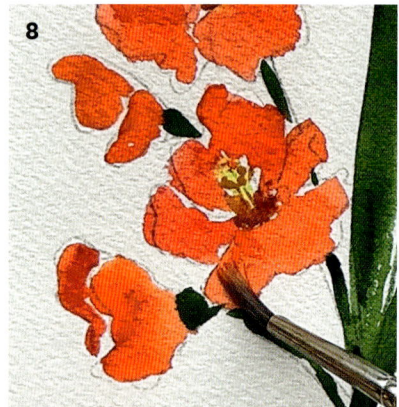
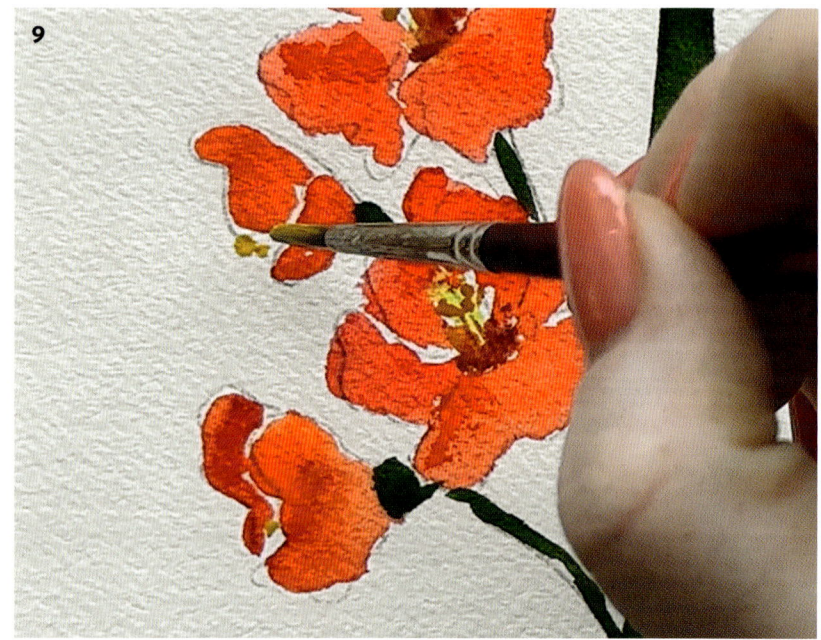

POPPY

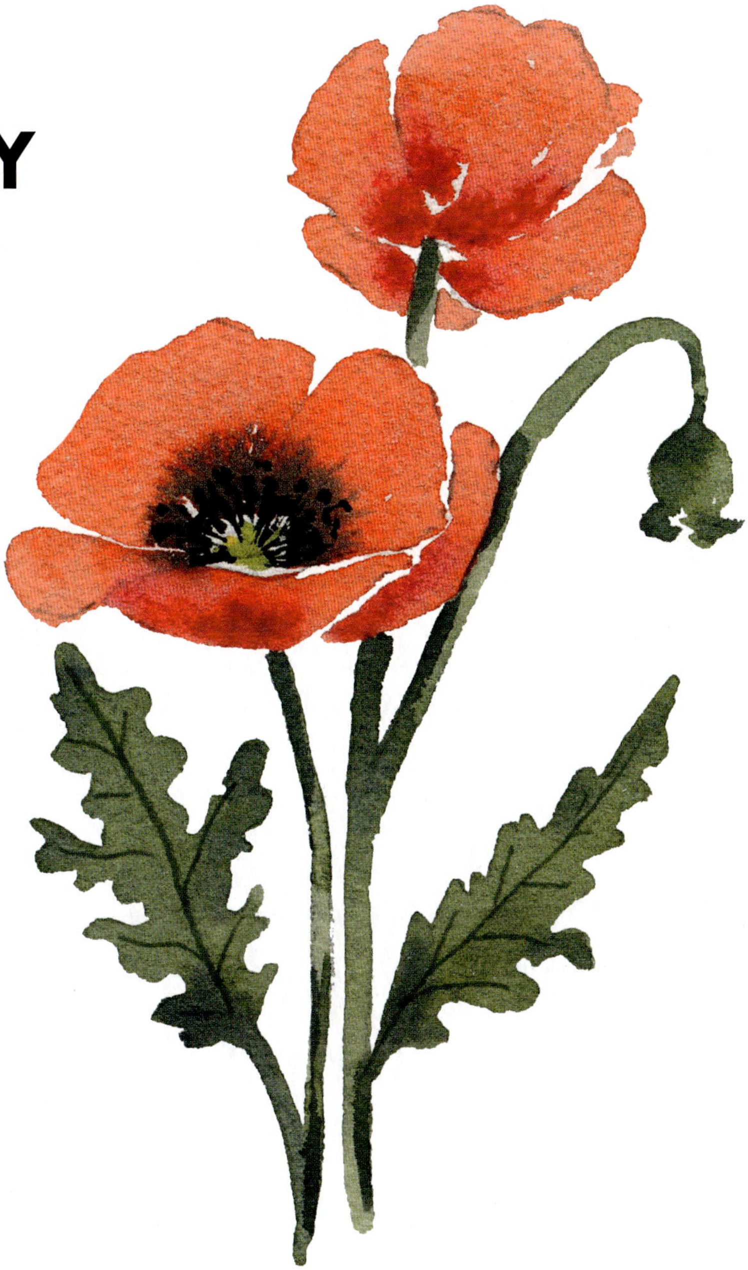

 Cadmium-free red

 Ultramarine

 Lemon yellow

 Permanent rose

 Cadmium-free yellow

 Cerulean

Scan the QR code to paint along.

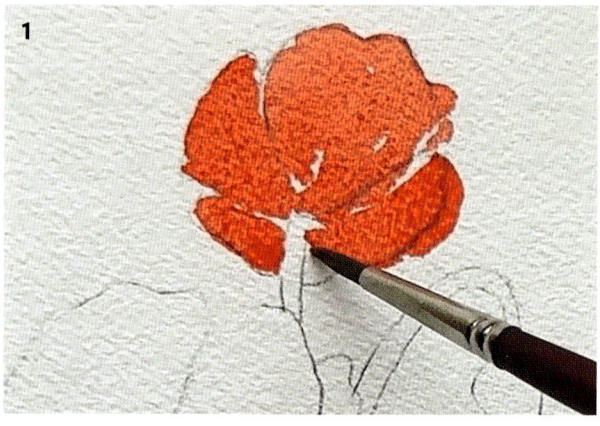

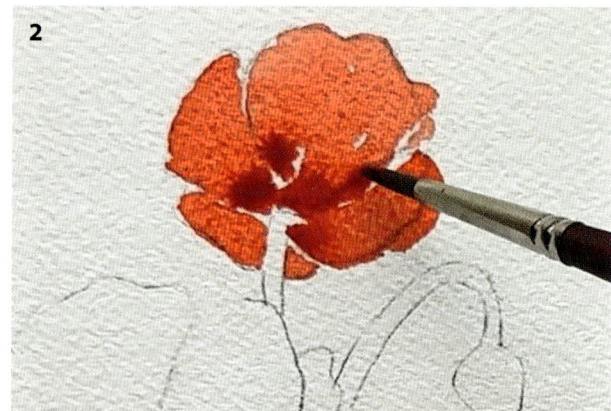

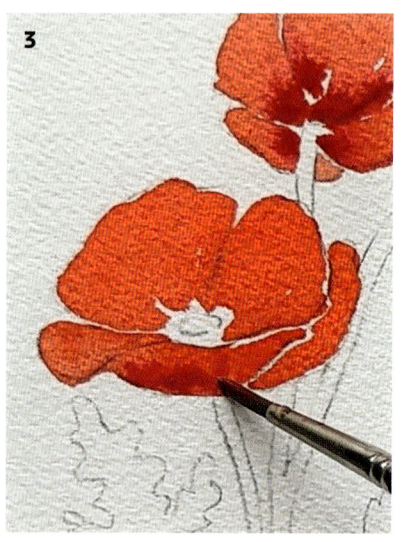

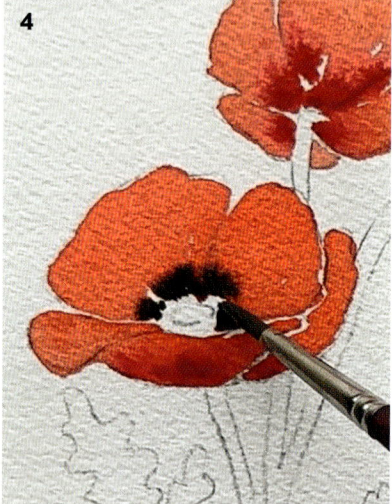

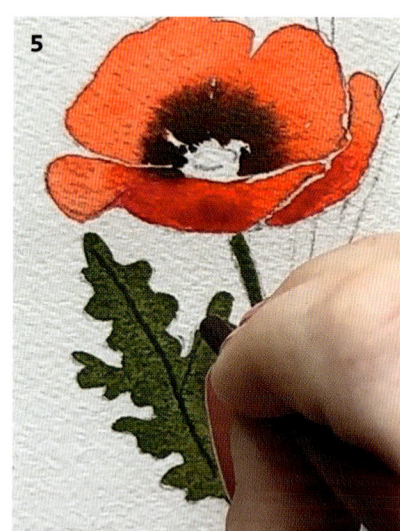

1 **Red petals:** Mix cadmium-free red and permanent rose to get a bright red wash. Paint petals around the stem and leave a bit of white space between the petals to keep them individually defined.

2 **Dark pink blends:** While the red petals are still wet, tap in a thick dark value of permanent rose at the base of the petals near the stem. This will add a slight blend for dimension.

3 **Dark pink shadows:** Add more permanent rose on the outside of the bottom petal while the red color is still wet. This will give a dark bleed into the petal, creating a natural shadow.

4 **Black centers:** While the red color is still wet, mix ultramarine and cadmium-free yellow into the red mixture on the palette to create a dark color close to black. Add this color to the bottom of the petals at the center of the poppy. If your petals are dry and the black doesn't blend in, soften the edge with water so it blends into the center.

5 **Greenery:** Mix cadmium-free yellow, lemon yellow, cerulean, and ultramarine until you have a deep blue green wash. Place that on one poppy stem and its leaf. Use the end of the paintbrush to push vein lines into the leaf.

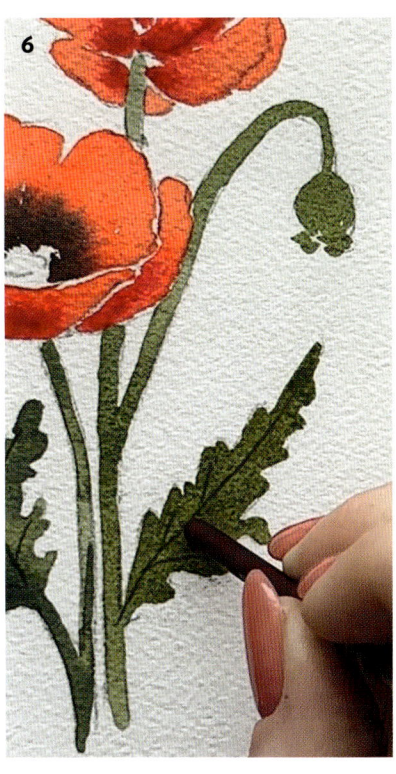

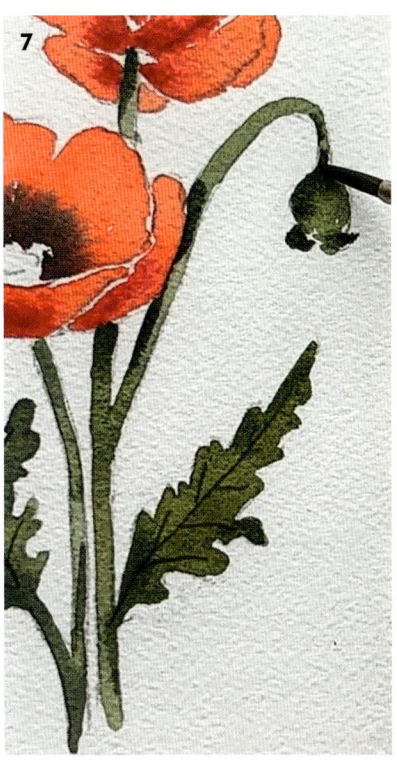

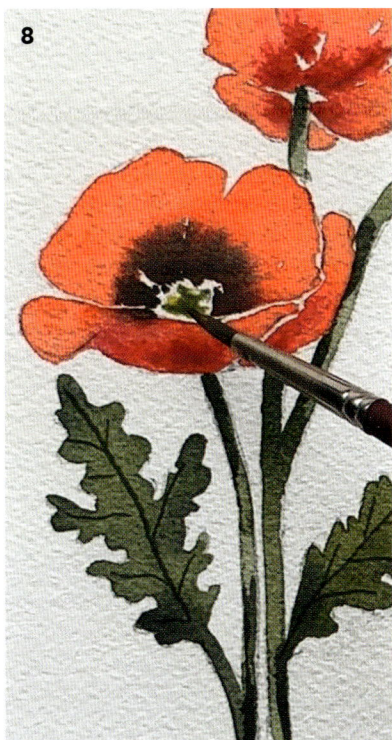

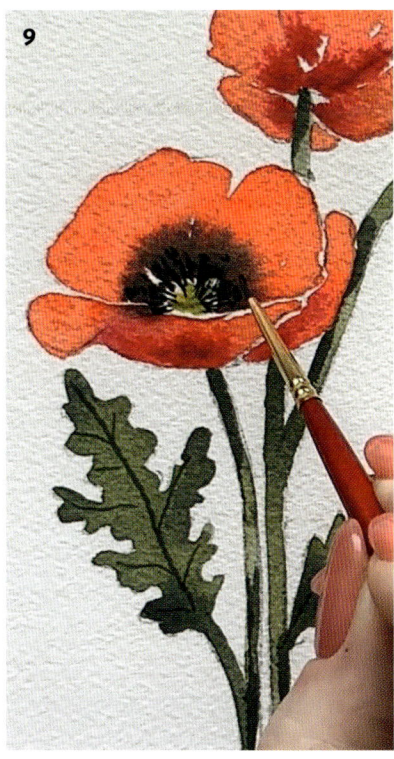

6 **Greenery shadows:** Use a more pigmented wash of ultramarine and mix it into the green you made previously on your palette. Tap this darker color into the leaf while it's still wet to create some interesting bleeds that give dimension to the leaf. Repeat steps 5 and 6 on remaining greenery. Push vein line impressions into the leaf.

7 **Deeper greenery shadows:** Add the deep ultramarine-green mix to the greenery in a few areas while the paint is still wet to give depth and create shadows.

8 **Yellow-green centers:** Mix a tiny bit of lemon yellow and the green on your palette until you get a bright yellow-green. Dot this color roughly into the center of the poppy, leaving some white of the paper.

9 **Black center details:** Once the center of the poppy is completely dry, use your smallest brush to dip into your previously mixed black. Add small lines from the green center out into the black bleed in the petals. Finish off the center with small dots at the end of the lines.

ASTER

 Cadmium-free yellow

 Ultramarine

 Permanent rose

 Sap green

 Burnt sienna

 *Scan the QR code to paint along.*

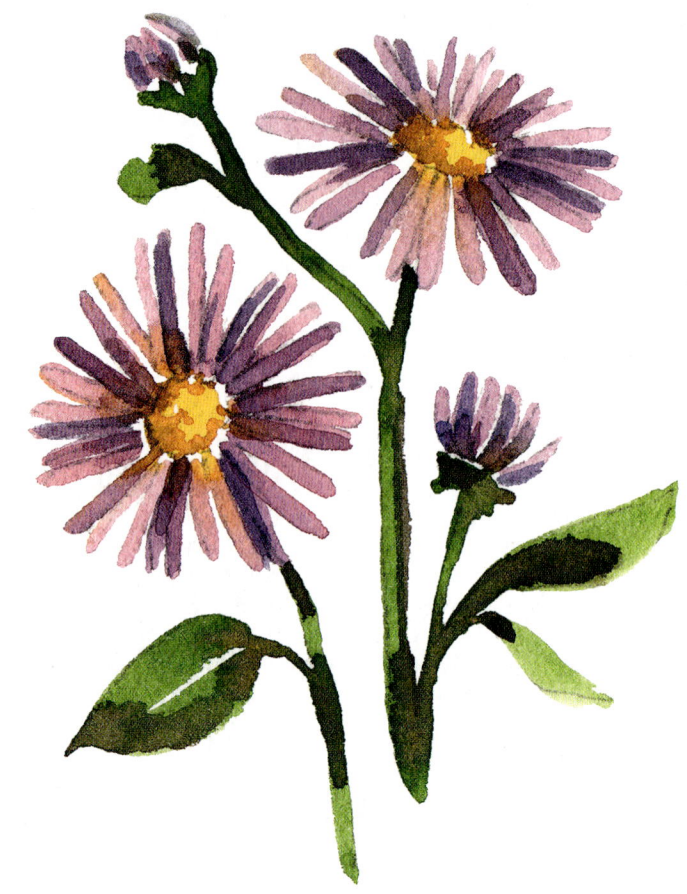

1 **Flower centers:** Add a wash of cadmium-free yellow to the centers of each of the open flowers.

2 **Petal base color:** Mix ultramarine and permanent rose to get a bright purple color. Starting at the center of the flower, push down slightly into the body of the brush and drag it to get the flower petals. I like how it looks when the center yellow color blends into some of the petals, but be careful not to let them blend too much since purple and yellow are complementary colors and will mute each other. The petals of asters are thin and there are a lot of them, so tuck them in all together, but don't worry too much about layering at this point. They can connect and merge together toward the center of the flower right now.

3 **Petal variations:** Mix permanent rose and ultramarine to get a deeper purple color. While the petals are still wet, tap this deeper color toward the yellow center, making sure not to tap any into the center so that the petals get most of the bleeds. You can also add more ultramarine to get an even darker color and paint a few of the petals with harder lines. Paint the small buds the light purple wash, then add deeper colors as it begins to dry.

4 **Greenery base color:** Mix sap green and cadmium-free yellow to create a bright green wash for the base of the greenery. Work in sections so that everything stays wet and this color can fill in the main stem, leaves, and other green details.

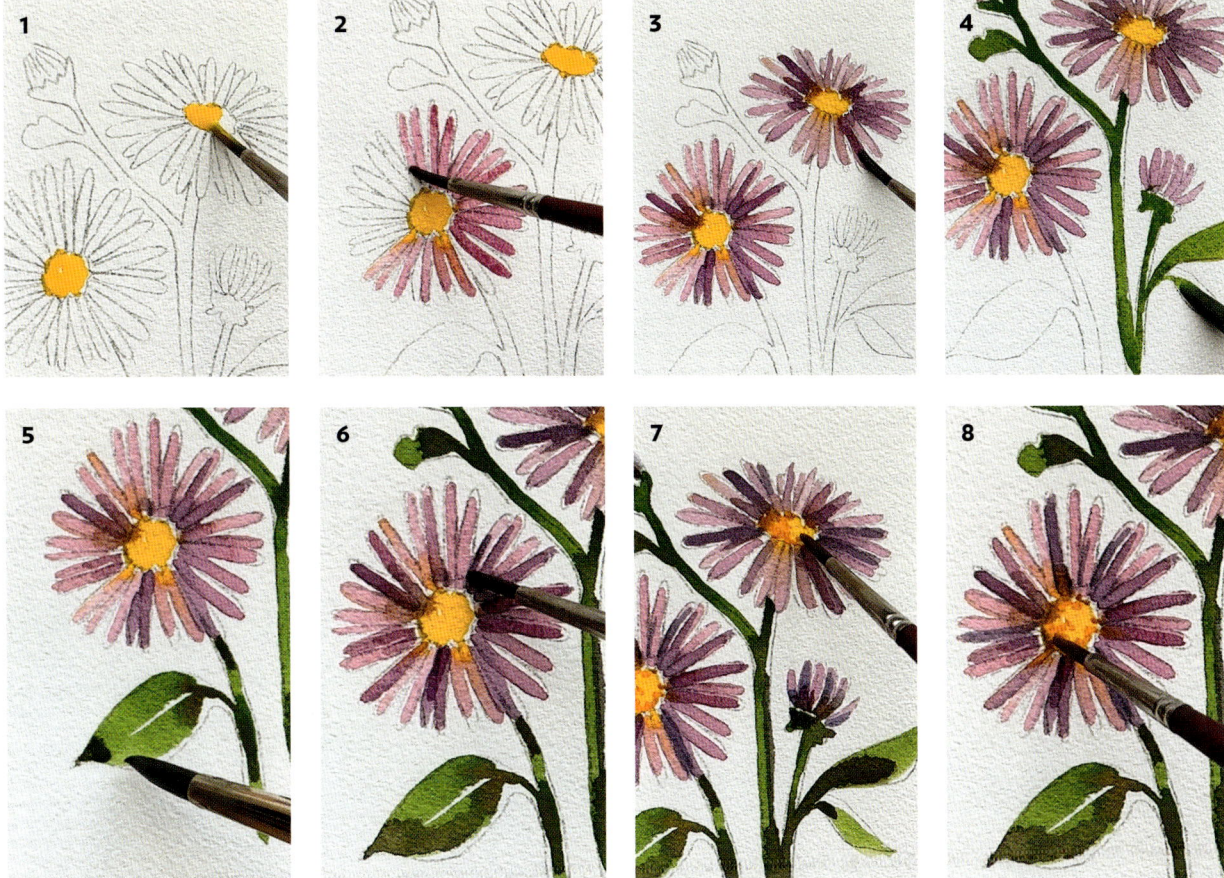

5 Greenery shadows: Add permanent rose, ultramarine, and cadmium-free yellow to your green mixture to get a deeper green color for the shadows. Tap this color in while the base green is still wet, at the points where the leaves and the stems meet. Think about where the natural shadows would be.

6 Deeper petal shadows: Mix ultramarine and permanent rose to get a deeper purple-blue color. Add layers on the buds and the petals. A little bit goes a long way, so only do a few strokes. Add more permanent rose for an even deeper color. Use this to add more depth to the flowers, but keep it minimal so the light and medium values remain visible.

7 Center shadows: Mix cadmium-free yellow and burnt sienna to create a deep orange color. Apply this color on one side of the center, keeping it consistent among all of the open flowers. Dot and stipple the paint to create texture, leaving the brighter color in the center open.

8 Deeper center shadows: Add more burnt sienna with a touch of the dark green mixture on the palette to the orange mixture to deepen the color and create a darker contrast for the center. Again, dot and stipple this color to create texture. Keep it very focused on one side, making sure not to overtake the medium value of orange from the previous step.

MORNING GLORY

 Lemon yellow

 Cadmium-free yellow

 Permanent rose

 Ultramarine

 Cerulean

 Sap green

 *Scan the QR code to paint along.*

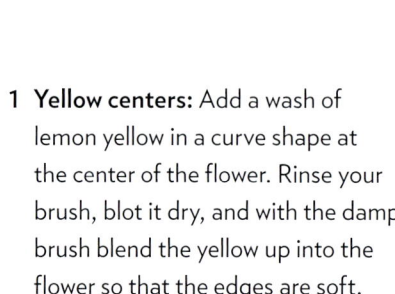

1 **Yellow centers:** Add a wash of lemon yellow in a curve shape at the center of the flower. Rinse your brush, blot it dry, and with the damp brush blend the yellow up into the flower so that the edges are soft.

2 **Center shadows:** Mix cadmium-free yellow and permanent rose for a deep orange color. While the center yellow color is still wet, place the orange directly at that curved edge to create depth within the trumpet of the flower to look like a shadow.

3 **Blue petals:** Pick up a medium wash of ultramarine and cerulean and outline the shape of the flower. Rinse your brush, blot it dry, and with a damp brush smooth out the inner edge of the blue wash so that it is light and blended out into the rest of the flower, creating a soft edge. Add more blue to the edge while still wet.

4 **Petal veins:** While the blue color is still wet, use the hard end of your brush to very gently press into the paper from the outer edge of the petal toward the center, creating a slight indentation for the paint to flow into. Make sure to curve this line with the shape of the flower in the direction that it would naturally be going toward the center.

5 **Side petals:** To paint the flower from the side, start with a wiggly long stroke to represent the flat top part of the flower, bringing that color down into a triangular shape for the trumpet portion of the flower. Mix ultramarine and

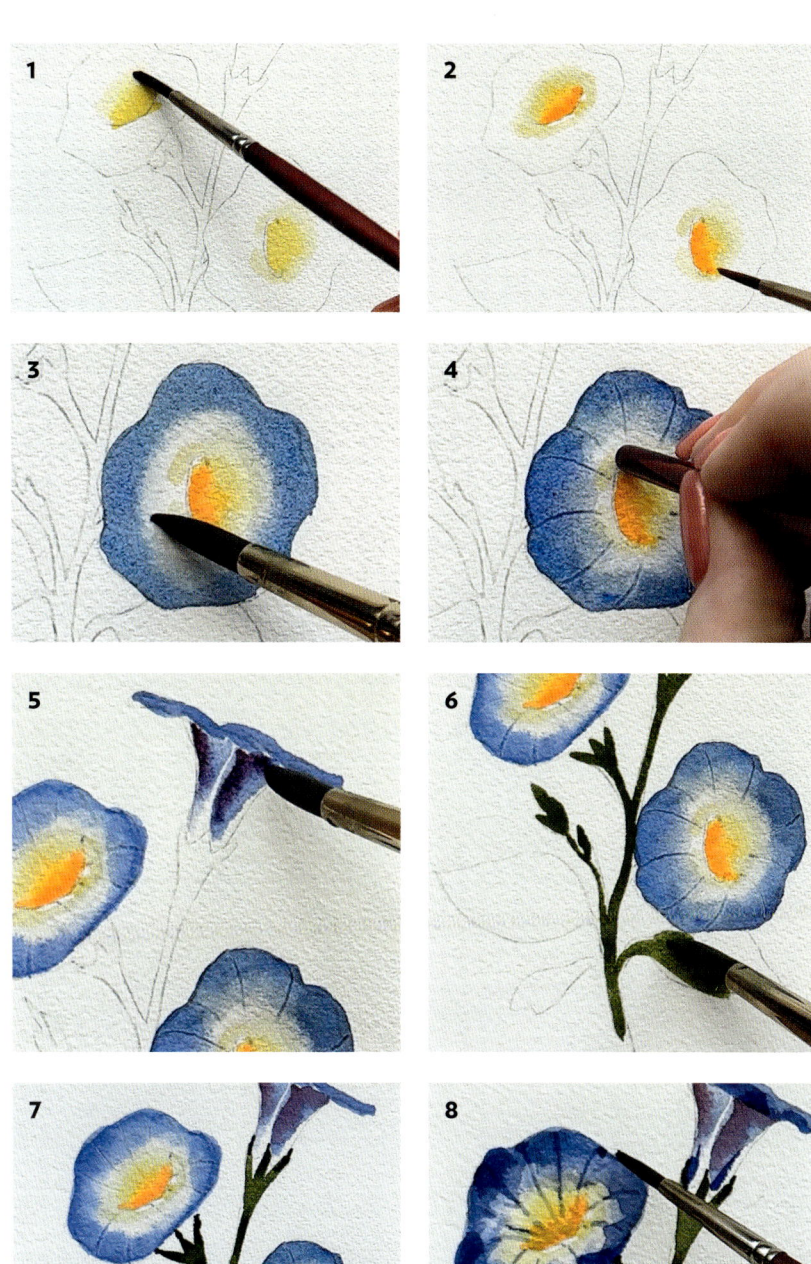

magenta to get a deeper purple blue. While the paint is still wet, create some shadow by tapping the darker blue in the triangular section.

6 **Greenery base color:** Mix sap green, ultramarine, and cadmium-free yellow for the base color of the greenery and add that to the leaves and the stems.

7 **Greenery shadows:** Mix more ultramarine and permanent rose into the green mixture to get a deeper shadow color. While the base greenery is still wet, tap the darker green in a few key places, especially where the leaves connect to the stem and other naturally shadowy places.

8 **Petal shadows:** Once the paper is dry, add more ultramarine to your petal mixture to build up the color and texture on the edges of the flowers. Add even more ultramarine for a deeper shade and add that along the petal edges and underneath the flat top of the side flower to achieve light, medium, and dark values. Sometimes a layer looks dark but then dries lighter, so don't be afraid to go back and continue adding depth, contrast, and darker layers until you feel satisfied.

OCTOBER

MARIGOLD

 Cadmium-free yellow

 Cadmium-free red

 Permanent rose

 Ultramarine

 Sap green

 *Scan the QR code to paint along.*

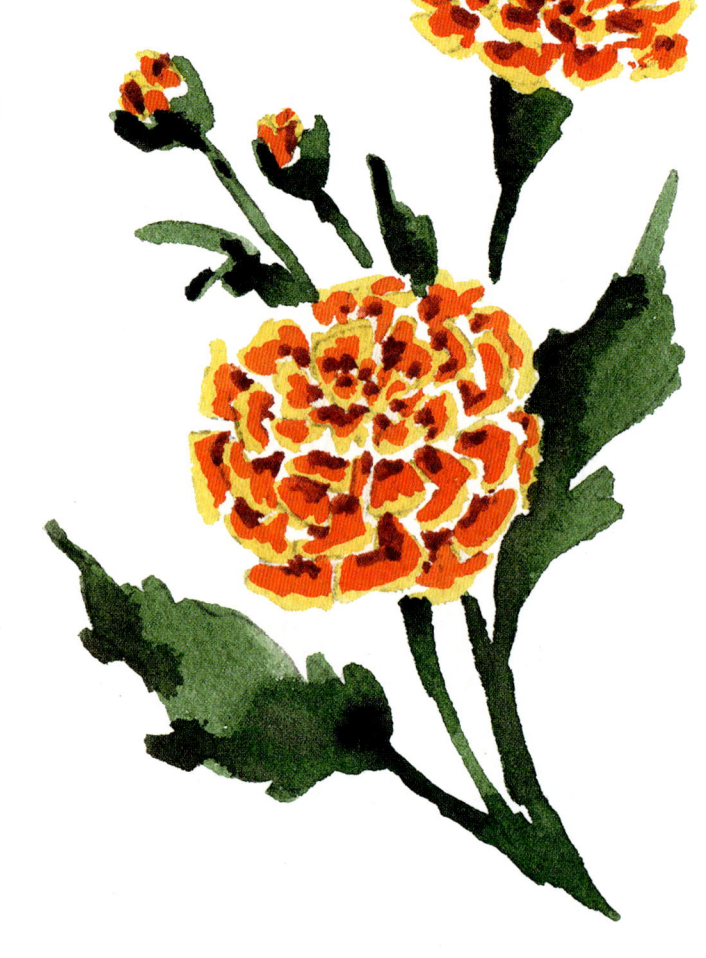

1 **Yellow layer:** Use cadmium-free yellow to create square shapes that tuck into each other around the flower. Leave some white space to distinguish between the petals. This yellow is the outline color of the petal. For the flower buds, roughly place some yellow color to give the impression that the petals are tucked into each other. Flowers that are seen from the side have some of the square shapes going in different directions than when viewed from the top.

2 **Red layer:** Mix cadmium-free red with a little bit of permanent rose for the main color of the petal. Starting at the base of the petal where it connects to the center, roughly fill in the yellow squares, leaving a yellow tip at the end.

3 **Buds and side flowers:** For the buds and flowers that are seen from the side, don't worry so much about the exactness of the square shapes but more on the solidness of the red color while also leaving an edge of yellow.

4 **Greenery base color:** Mix ultramarine and sap green to get a deep green base color. Paint the stems and leaves.

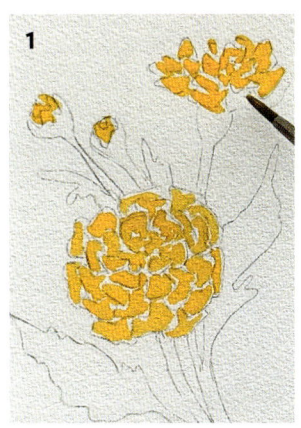
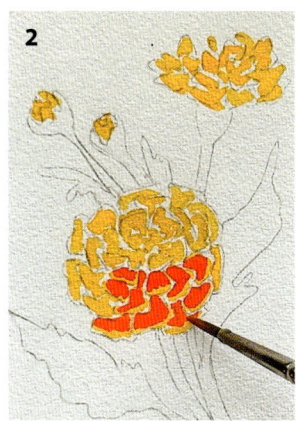
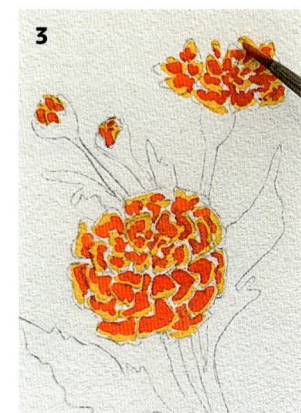
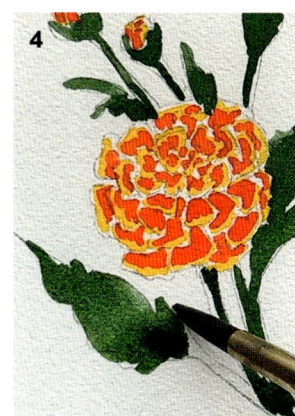

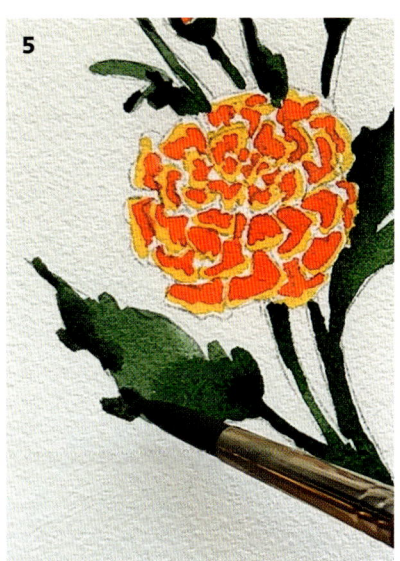
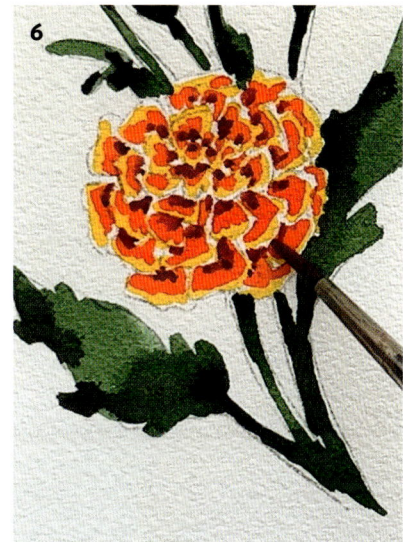
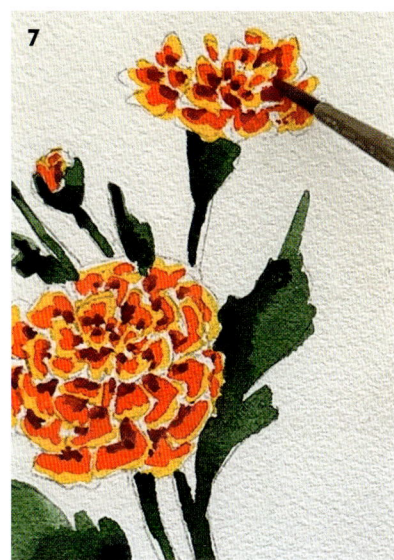

5 Greenery shadows: Add more ultramarine and a touch of permanent rose to your green mixture to get a deeper green for the shadows. While the base color is still wet, apply this color on one side consistently throughout the painting. Move quickly so that you get a nice gradual bleed, but some hard lines are also nice. If you want to soften the edges, rinse your brush, blot it dry, and with the damp brush blend the color out to look like a natural bleed.

6 Petal shadows: Mix permanent rose, cadmium-free red, and a bit of ultramarine to get a deep burgundy for the shadows on the petals. Place this shadow color right at the base of the petal where it meets the center.

7 Buds and side flowers: Add a small amount of the dark red color to the base of the buds. Use a light hand so this color is not the main focus and blend it out with a damp brush if the lines are too hard.

COSMOS

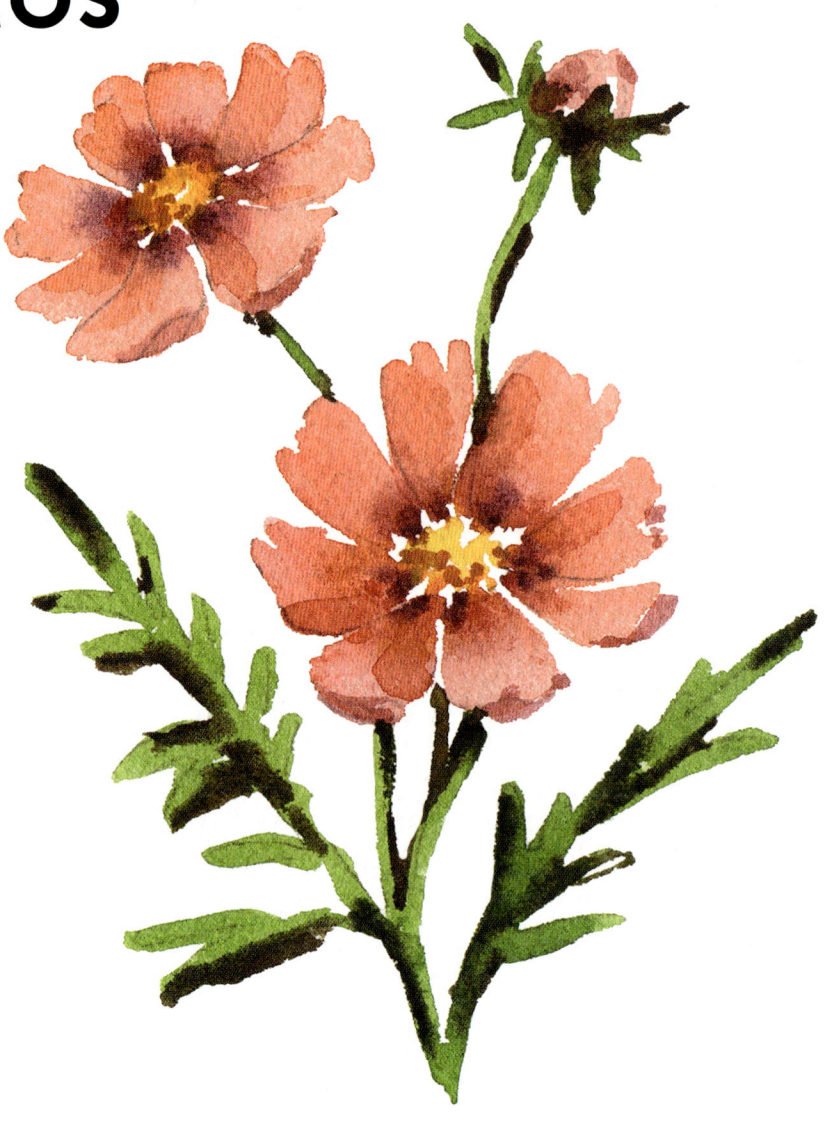

 Permanent rose

 Ultramarine

 Sap green

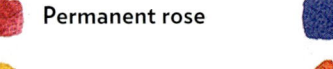 **Cadmium-free yellow**

 Cadmium-free red

 Burnt sienna

 *Scan the QR code to paint along.*

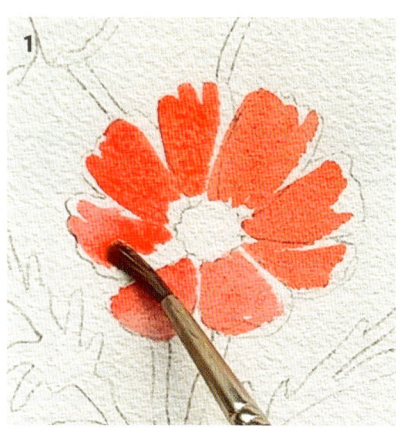
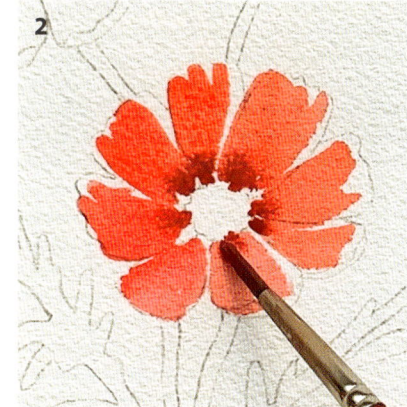
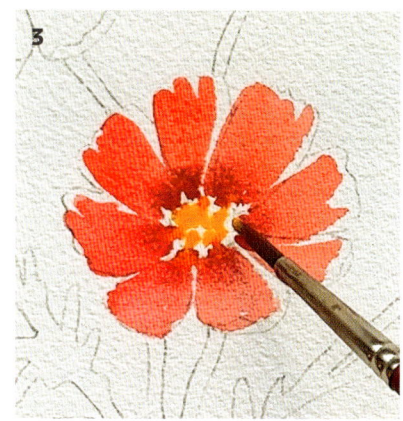

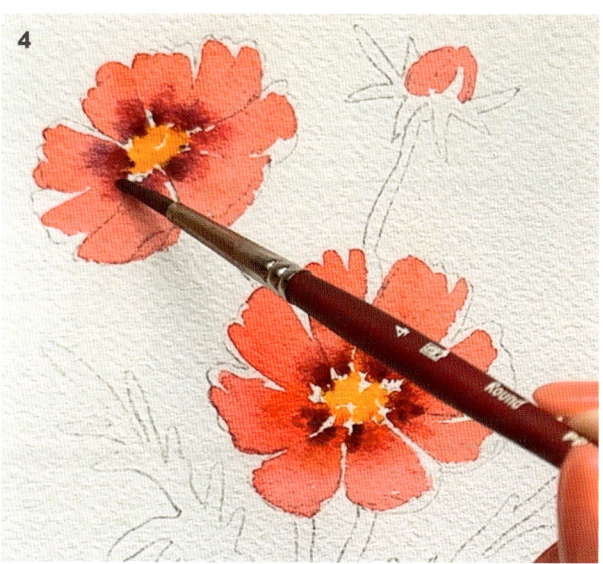
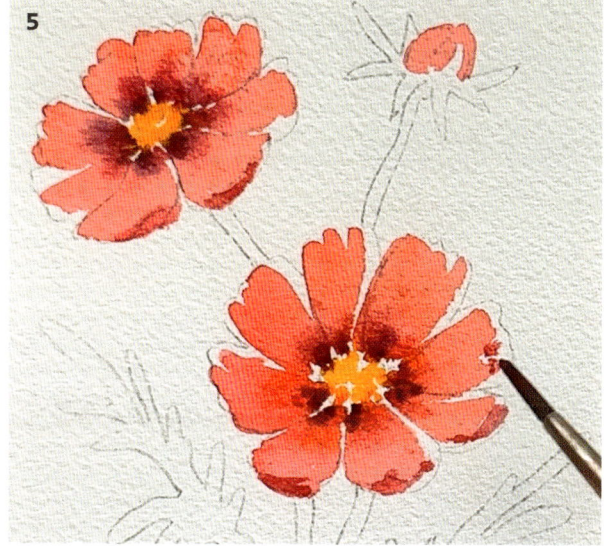

1 **Petal base color:** Mix a light wash of permanent rose and cadmium-free yellow. Use the tip of your brush to create a rough, uneven edge of the petal, bringing the color down to the center but leaving the center open. Leave some slight gaps for definition between the petals and keep the edges rough.

2 **Petal details:** Mix a more concentrated magenta with a bit of ultramarine and cadmium-free red. While the initial base color for the petals is still wet, add this darker color around the base of the petals at the center, giving it a slight bleed.

3 **Flower centers:** Use a light wash of cadmium-free yellow for the center. Dot and stipple the color in to give it a textured look.

4 **Deeper petal details:** Add more ultramarine to the magenta mixture on your palette to get a darker, more purple color and add that at the base of the petals in the center.

5 **Petal shadows:** Add some water to the darker magenta color and make a quick, uneven swipe at the edge of petals where you want to turn up the edges.

6 **Greenery base color:** Mix sap green and cadmium-free yellow to get a light base green color. Paint thin stems, the sepals around the bud, and long scraggly leaves using the shape of your brush.

7 **Greenery shadows:** Add more ultramarine and permanent rose into your green mixture for a deep shadow green color. Add this color to one side consistently throughout all your greenery and underneath the flowers.

8 **Deeper petal shadows:** Mix burnt sienna and cadmium-free yellow to get a deep orange color. Add this color on the same side of the center that you added your greenery shadows. Dot the color in to give it texture and use a light hand so that the bright yellow center is still visible.

9 **Final glaze:** Add water to permanent rose that you have on your palette to create a light glaze. Use this wash over some areas on the petals, creating dimension and texture. Make sure that the light, medium, and dark values are visible.

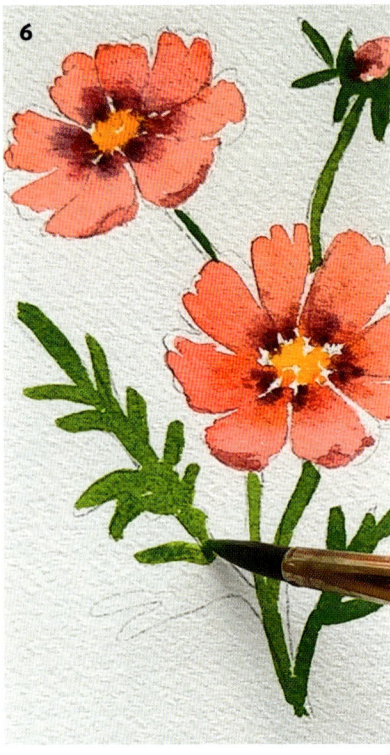
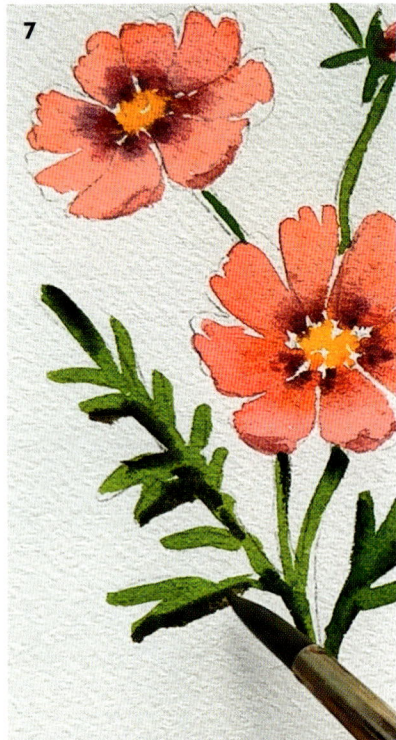
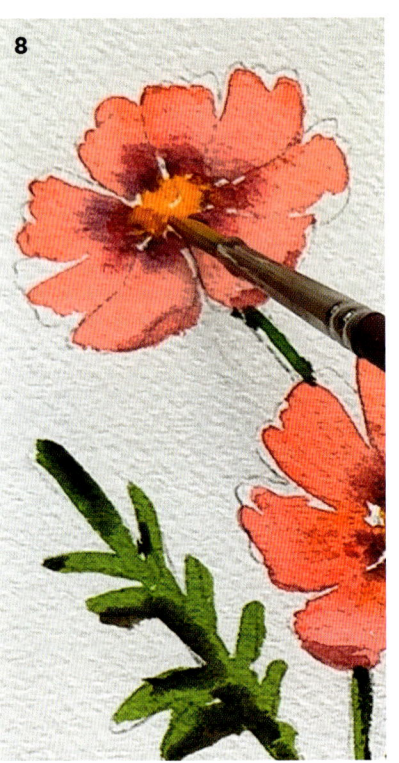
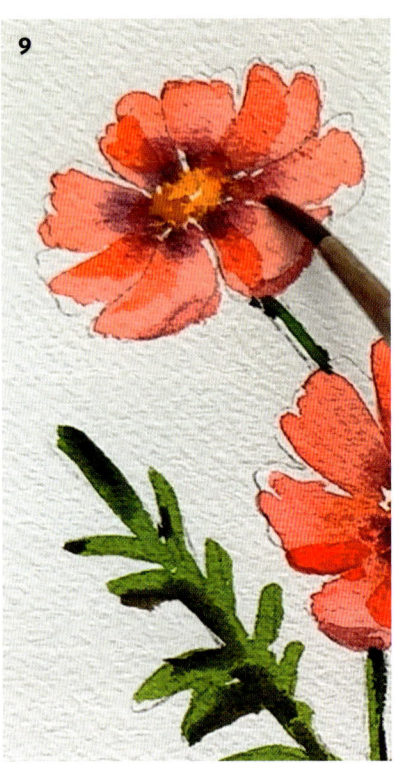

CHRYSANTHEMUM

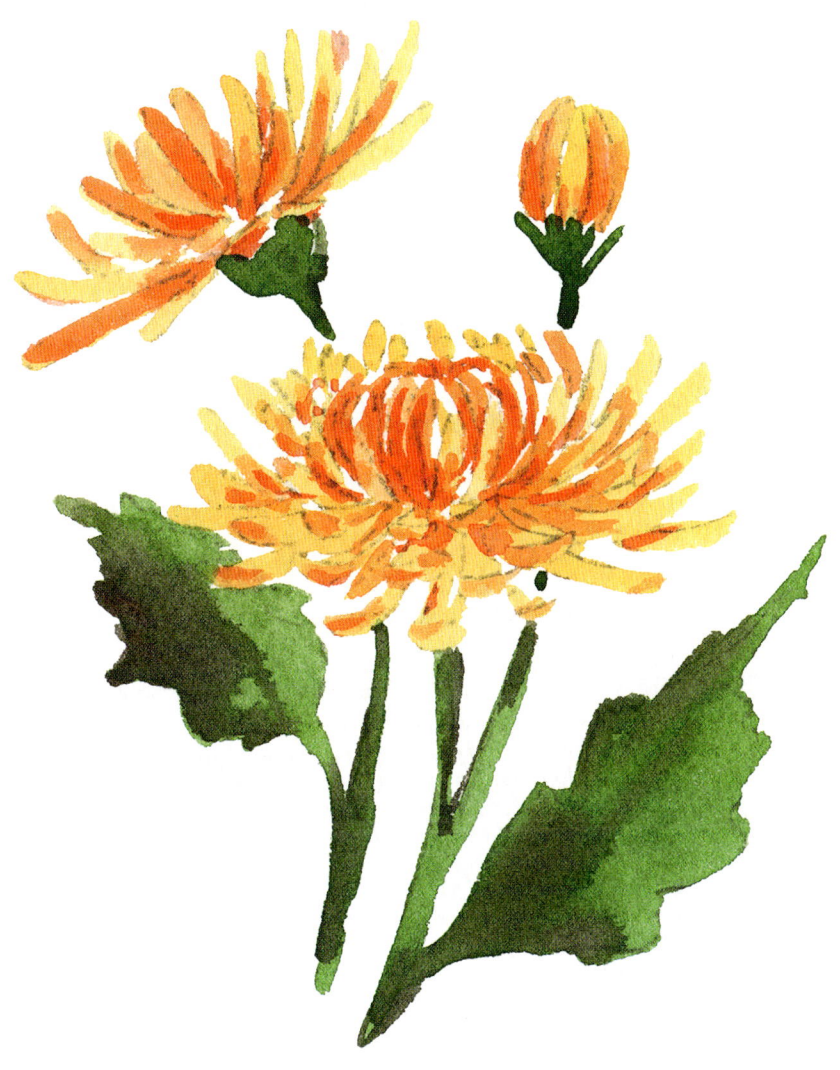

 Cadmium-free yellow

 Cadmium-free red

 Lemon yellow

 Permanent rose

 Sap green

 Ultramarine

 *Scan the QR code to paint along.*

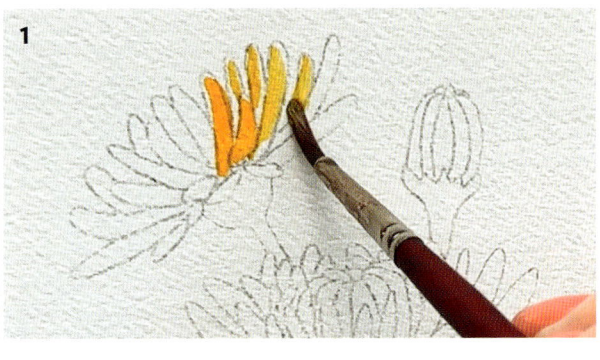

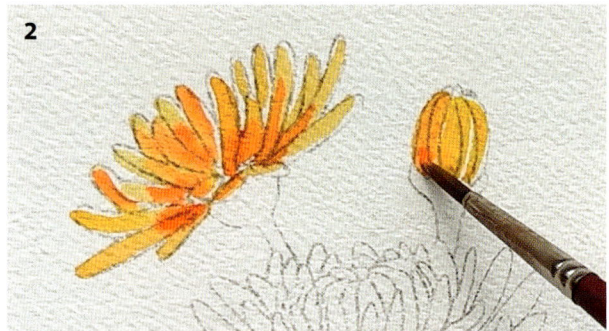

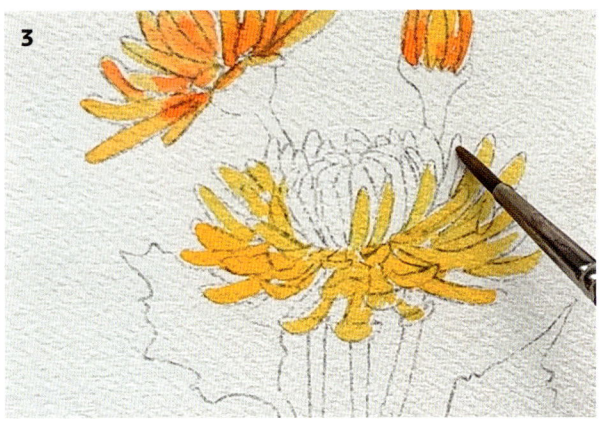

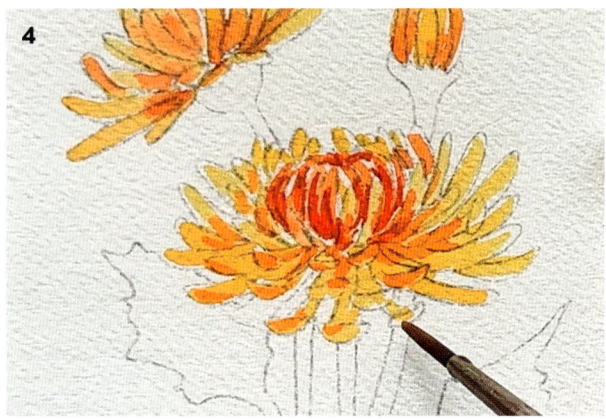

1 **Yellow petals:** Mix cadmium-free yellow with a bit of cadmium-free red to get a bright yellow-orange color. To paint the flower from the side, curve the petals down from the top into the connection point at the stem, using the shape of your brush to create lots of long petals that are tucked into each other. Leave some white space for petal separation. Use lemon yellow on some petals to create brighter areas.

2 **Orange petals:** Add more cadmium-free red to the mixture on your palette to create an even more concentrated orange color.

While the petals are still wet, tap in the darker orange at the base where the petals connect to the greenery. Paint the bud with the petals tucked into each other with the light orange-yellow color, leaving a tiny bit of white space for petal separation. Then add the darker orange at the base while everything is still wet.

3 **Main flower:** For the main chrysanthemum flower, paint some petals curving from the top down and in using the yellow-orange color. Using the same color, paint the petals that are pointed outward, so they are long on the

sides with flat, almost teardrop shapes at the tip.

4 **Flower center:** Use the darker orange from step 2 to paint the center petals. These petals are a lot more tucked into each other, similar to the bud, so maintain a bit of white space to help differentiate between them. Add a bit more cadmium-free red to the dark orange mixture on your palette and add this color on the tips of the petals that are pointing toward you, at the base of the petals as they get closer to the center, and on the outer petals on the bud.

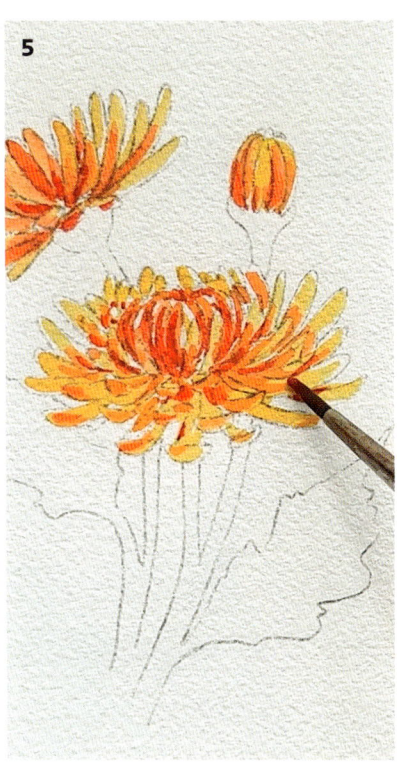

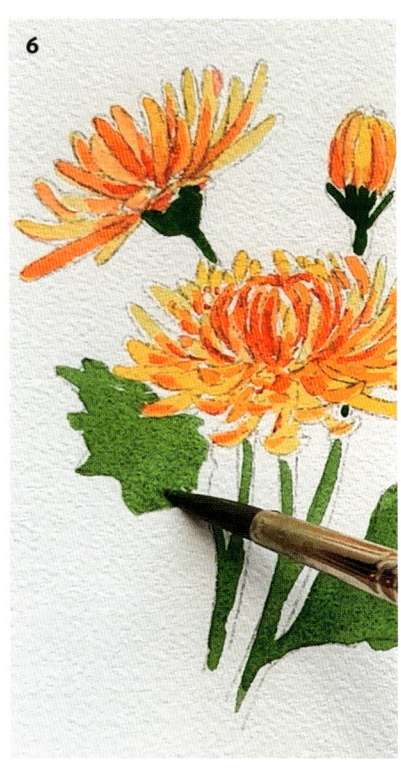

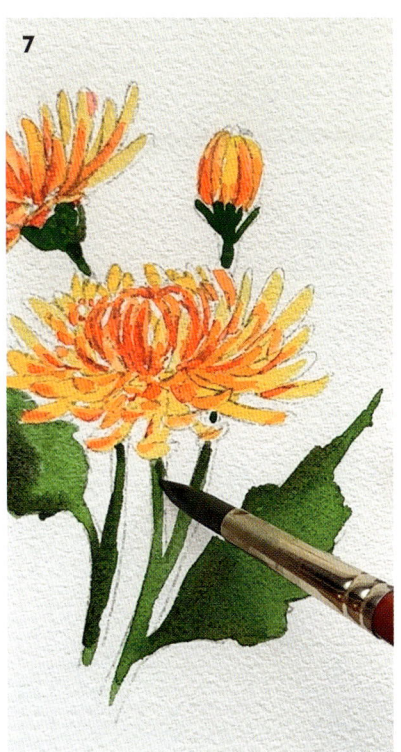

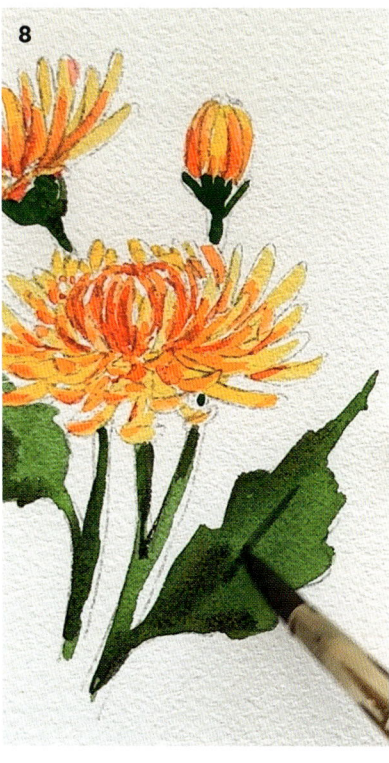

5 **Petal shadows:** Mix even more cadmium-free red and some permanent rose into the dark orange-red mixture on your palette to get a deeper red color. Add some of this deeper color on the center petals, leaving some of the medium values and white space, to get some deep shadows. Add a little bit of this color on the bud and on some of the petals on the upper-left flower.

6 **Greenery base color:** Mix sap green, ultramarine, and cadmium-free yellow for a light green base and paint the stems, leaves, and greenery with this color.

7 **Greenery shadows:** Add a bit more ultramarine with a bit of permanent rose into the green mixture to create a deep green color. Tap this into the leaves while the base color is still wet. Add the deeper green color on the stems where the flower is casting a shadow and on the connection points between the greenery and the top flowers.

8 **Leaf vein:** Add a thick center vein to the leaf on the right. Keep it simple because there is so much going on with the petals of the flower.

PEONY

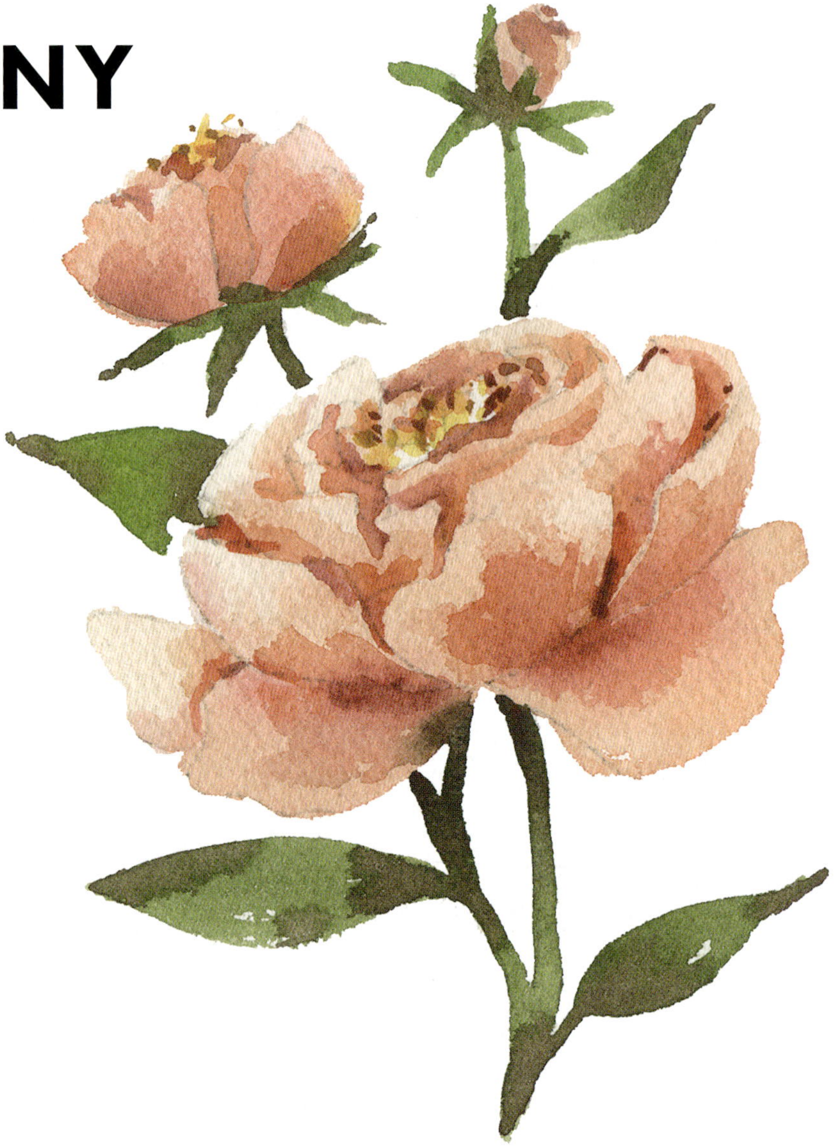

 Cadmium-free yellow

 Ultramarine

 Burnt sienna

 Permanent rose

 Sap green

Scan the QR code to paint along.

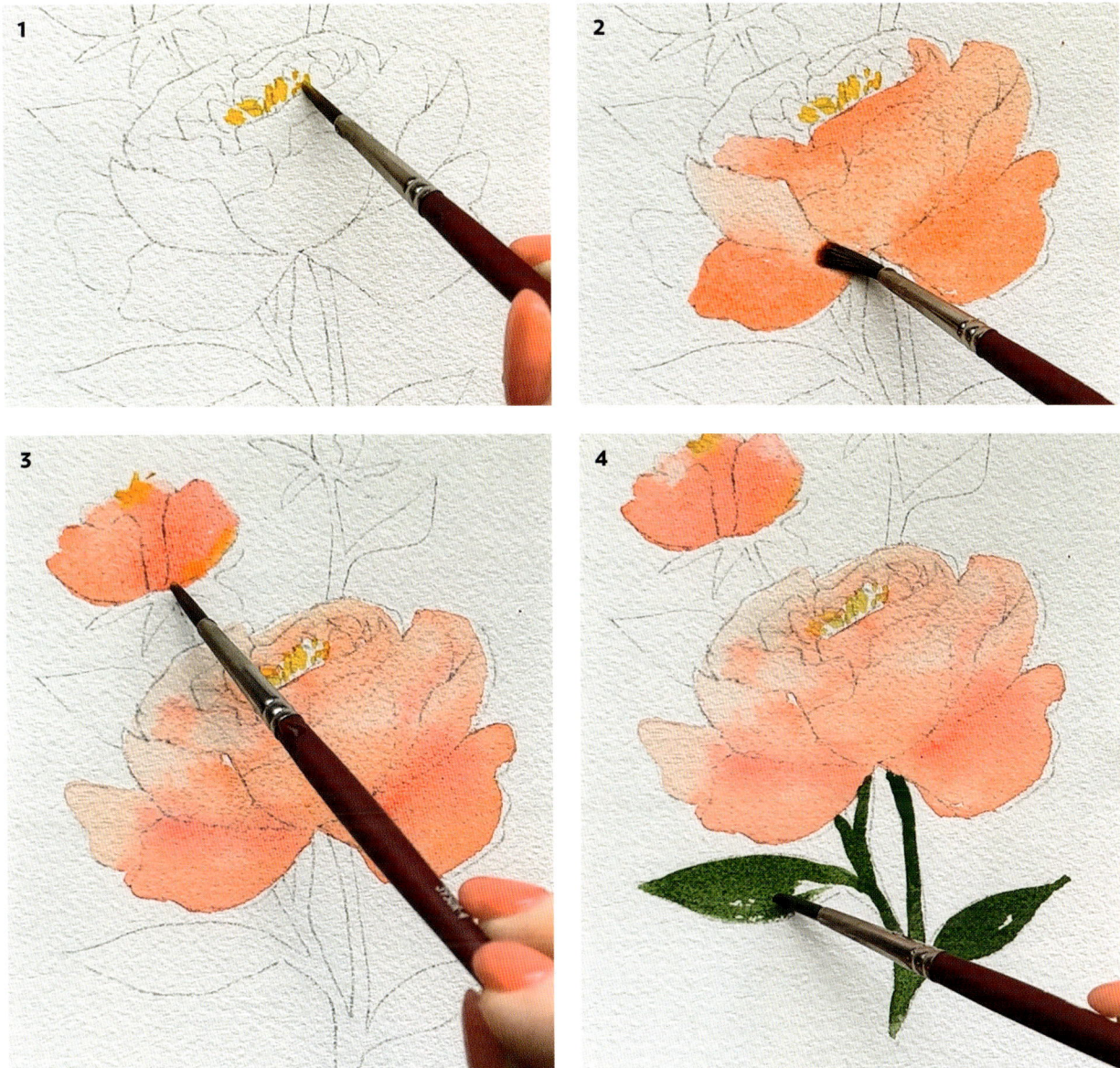

1 **Flower center:** Pick up a light cadmium-free yellow wash and paint some quick, short lines for the center stamen.

2 **Petal base color:** Mix cadmium-free yellow with permanent rose to get a warm orangey pink color. Fill in the petals on all the flowers.

3 **Petal variation:** While the base color is still wet, drop in more yellow or more magenta on some of the petals to create variation.

4 **Greenery base color:** Mix cadmium-free yellow, ultramarine, and sap green to get a deep green color and paint the stems and leaves with this color.

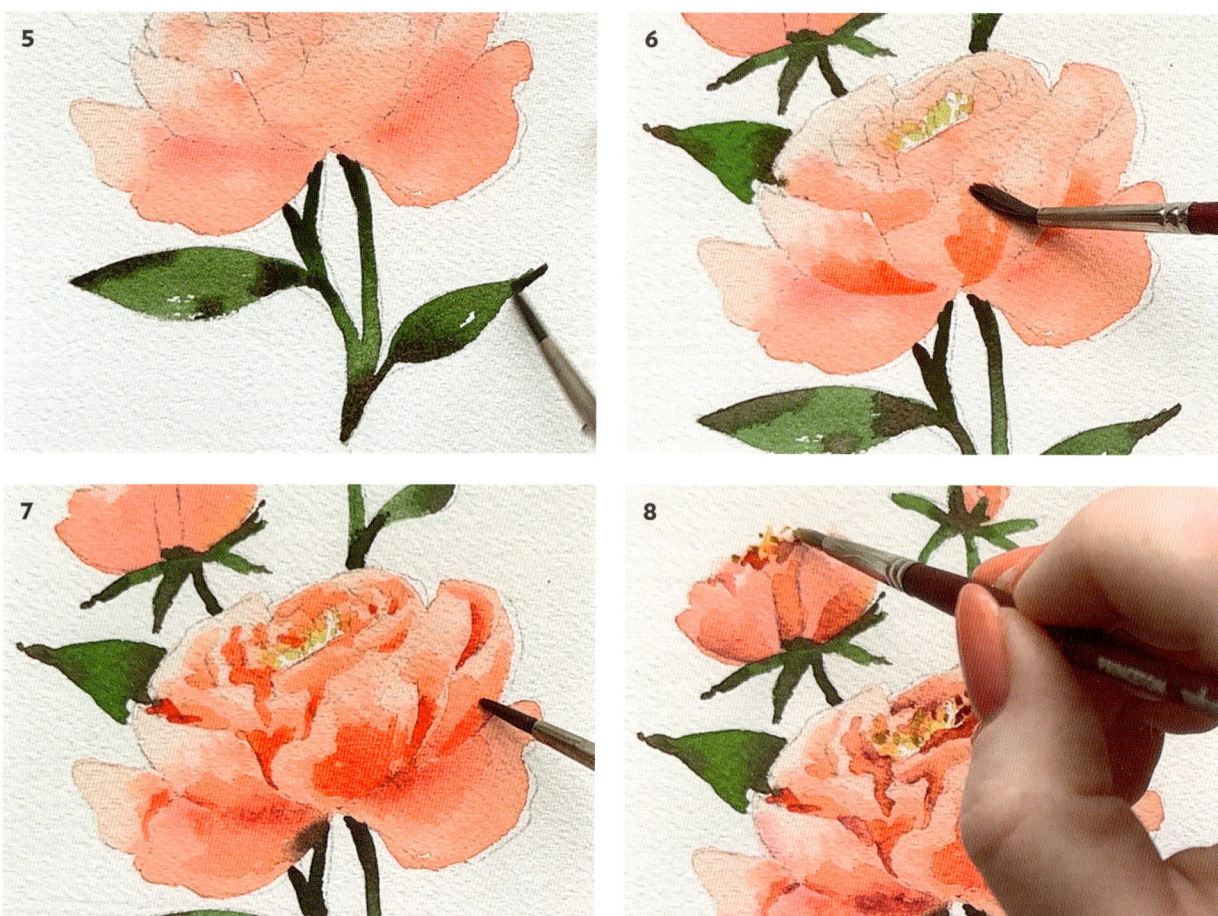

5 **Greenery shadows:** Add some more ultramarine and permanent rose into the green mixture on your palette to get a deep green for shadow. Add this color to the leaves and stems while they are still wet to get a nice natural bleed.

6 **Petal shadows:** Once the base layer of your peony is dry, mix cadmium-free yellow and permanent rose to get a more concentrated petal color. Add this color at the base of the petals.

Rinse your brush, blot it dry, and use the damp brush to blend out the edges up into the tips of the petals for a soft look.

7 **Deeper petal shadows:** While that blended pink is still wet, add a more concentrated wash of permanent rose in the areas where the petals meet. Then mix ultramarine into your pink mixture to get a darker pink and add this to the crevices to give the impression of tight shadows.

Continue adding lighter colors, blending them out, and adding punchier, deeper magenta into those colors while they are still wet to create depth within the petals.

Keep the tips of the petals light and focus the deeper colors at the base where the petals meet in the center.

8 **Stamen details:** Using a thick wash of cadmium-free yellow mixed with burnt sienna, add a few more dotted details for the stamen.

NARCISSUS
(PAPERWHITES)

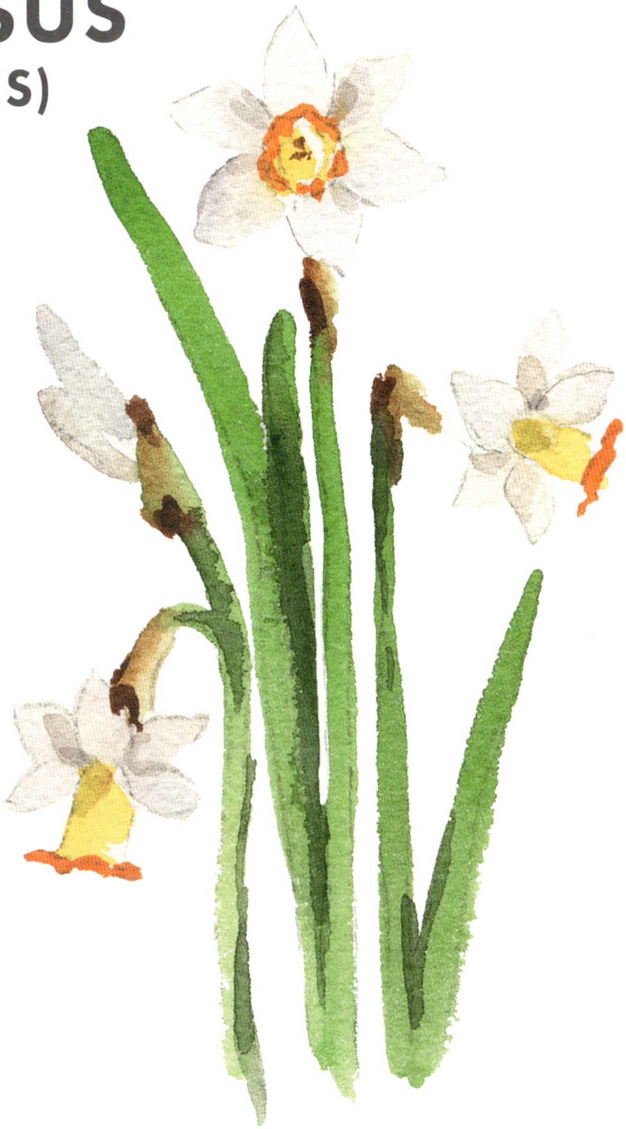

 Cadmium-free yellow

 Cadmium-free red

 Ultramarine

 Burnt sienna

Sap green

Scan the QR code to paint along.

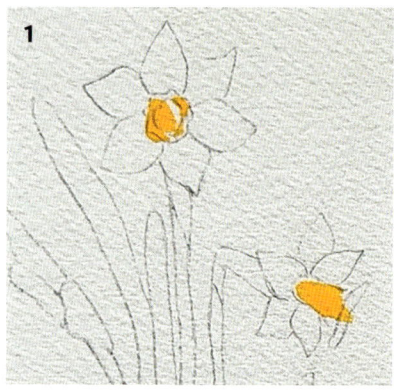
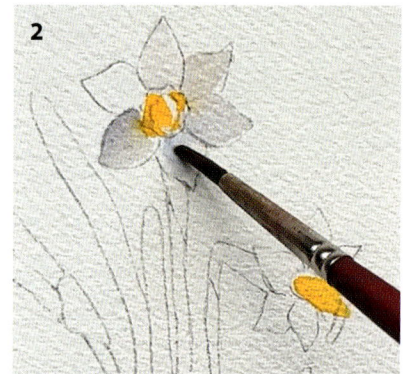
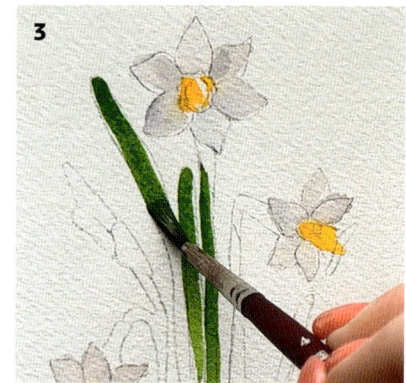

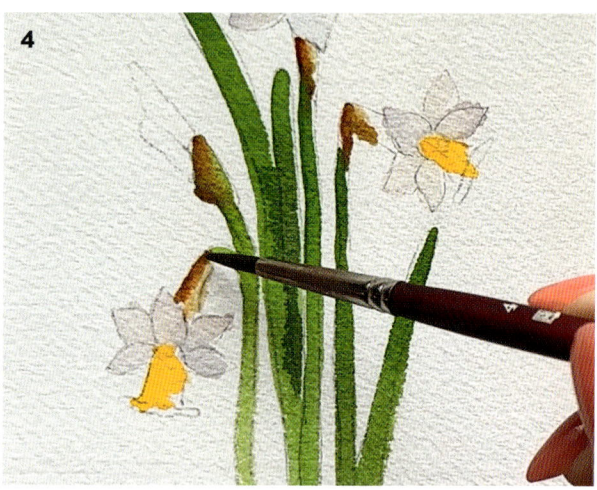
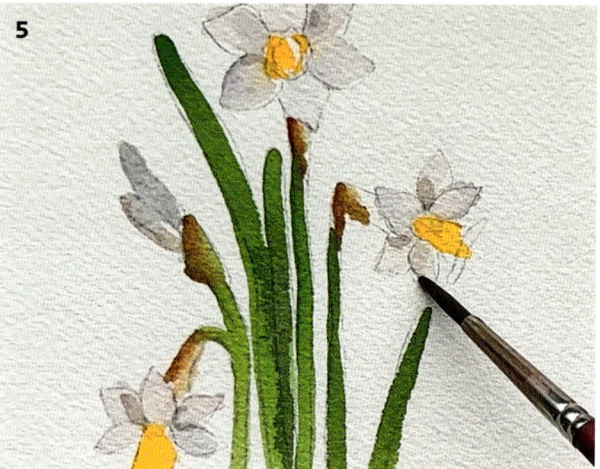

1 **Yellow trumpets:** Pick up a light wash of cadmium-free yellow and paint loose trumpet shapes in the center of the flowers. Leave a bit of white space for the colors to breathe. The flower that is facing out will just be a rough circle.

2 **Petal "white" color:** Mix a light wash of cadmium-free red, ultramarine, and burnt sienna to get a gray-purple color. Add lots of water to make sure this color is light because this is the color that you'll use to paint "white." Bring this color from the center of the flower into a curved triangle shape for the petals.

3 **Greenery base color:** Mix sap green and cadmium-free yellow to create a green mixture for the greenery. Using the shape of the smaller size 4 round brush, pull the stems and leaves down using the body of the brush.

4 **Tops of stems:** While the green is still wet, add a light wash of burnt sienna just at the top of the stems, but before you get to the thicker part of the stem that's attached to the flower. Leave some white space for highlights. Quickly rinse your brush, blot it dry, and use the damp brush to blend that color out ever so slightly into the thicker area just underneath the flower.

5 **Petal shadows:** Mix cadmium-free red and ultramarine for a slightly darker, grayish purple wash for shadows on the petals. Place this in a few spots in the flowers and the bud.

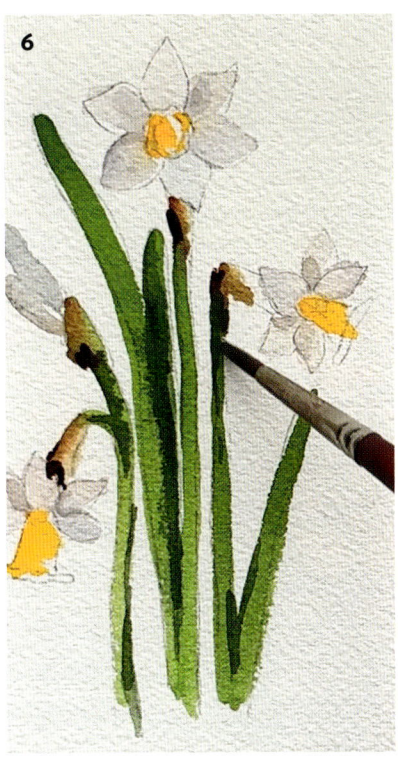

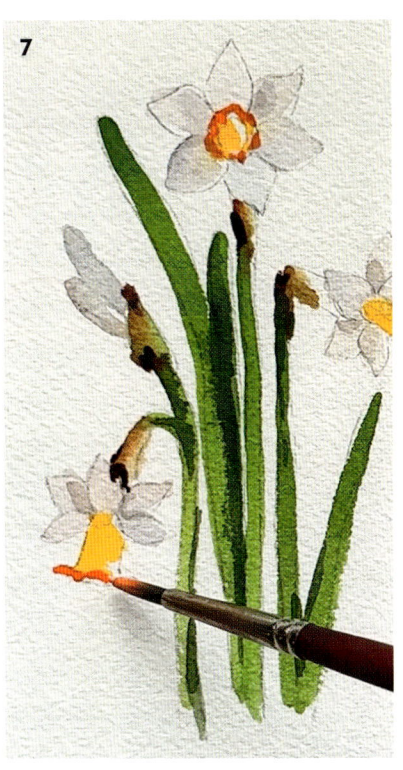

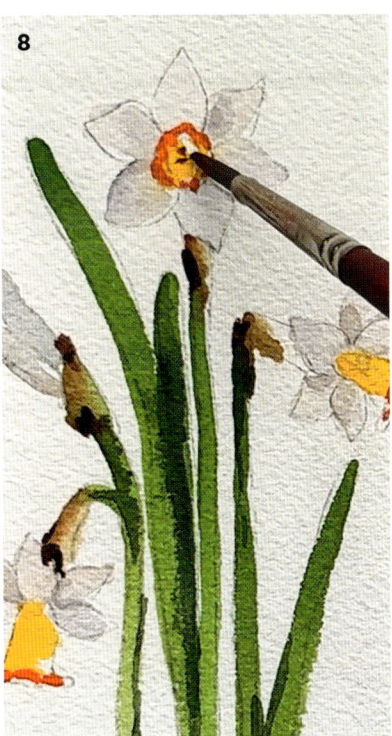

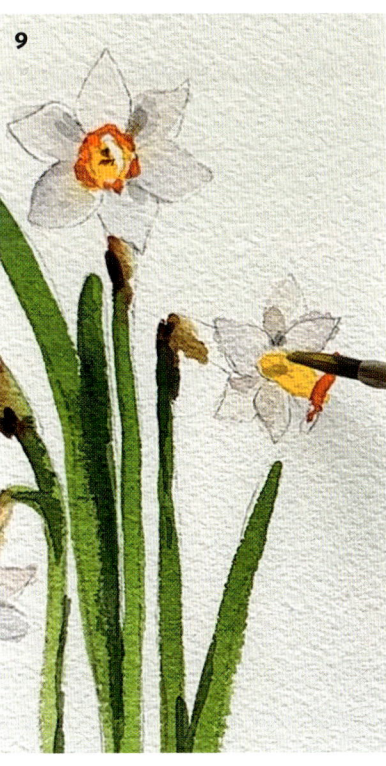

6 **Greenery shadows:** Add more ultramarine to the green mixture on your palette to get a deeper green. Add this to the leaves, stems, and connection points just under the flowers. Keep the bright green areas and don't overpower them with the darker green. Add a bit more ultramarine to your deep green color and paint a darker contrast on the stems just underneath the brown sections.

7 **Trumpet details:** Mix cadmium-free yellow and cadmium-free red to get a bright orange that leans into red. Use that color to create the rough edge of the trumpet on the flowers.

   Use a wiggly line for the flowers that you see from the side and a rough, not completely connected circle for the flower facing forward.

8 **Stamen details:** Pick up burnt sienna in a darker wash and add details where the flower meets the stem and make a few small dots in the center of the flower that is facing forward to give it the illusion of a stamen present.

9 **Deeper petal shadows:** Pick up a light wash of ultramarine and add a final shadow detail on the petals and at the base of the trumpets on each flower.

DECEMBER

HOLLY

 Sap green

 Cadmium-free yellow

 Ultramarine

 Burnt sienna

 Permanent rose

 Cadmium-free red

 *Scan the QR code to paint along.*

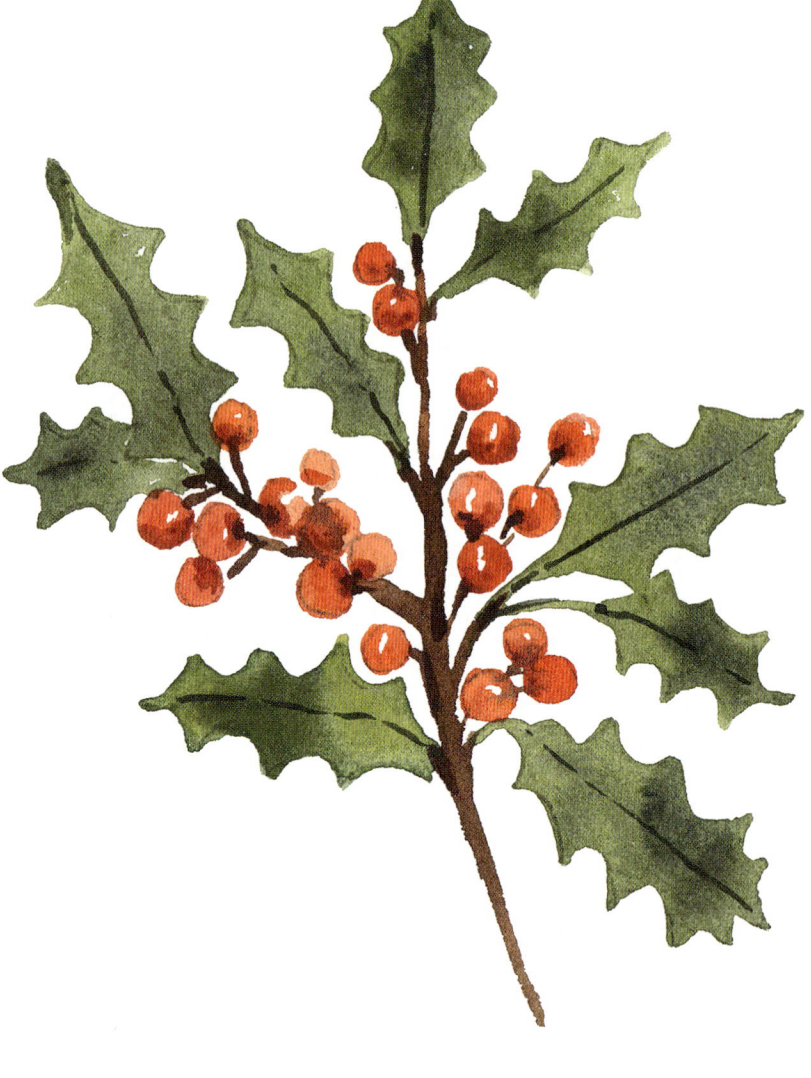

1 **Greenery base color:** Mix sap green, cadmium-free yellow, and ultramarine to get a deep green color for the leaves. Outline the edges first, starting at the top point and making three or four semicircles on one side and then repeating on the other side. Quickly fill in the center while the edges are still wet.

2 **Greenery shadows:** Add more ultramarine to the green mixture on your palette. While the green is still wet, drop in some of the deeper color for dimension within each leaf. Leave some white space between leaves that overlap so you can differentiate between them.

3 **Brown stems:** Mix burnt sienna, permanent rose, and ultramarine to get a deep brown color. Paint the main branch of the holly.

4 **Red berries:** Mix a bright wash of cadmium-free red with a touch of permanent rose. Form the circular shapes of the holly berries, keeping them closely bunched together. Leave small gaps in the paint to reveal the white of the paper to give the berries a slight shine.

5 Berry shadows: Add more permanent rose into the red mixture to get a deep red color. Place a bit of this color on each berry, hugging the edge.

6 Tiny branches: While the berries are still slightly damp, pick up the dark brown wash and paint in some tiny branches to connect them. This allows a slight dark brown bleed in some berries, creating a lot of shadow and dimension.

7 Branch shadows: Add a bit more ultramarine to the brown mixture and paint this darker color around the main branch and within the berry stems for more contrast.

8 Leaf veins: Add more ultramarine to the green color on your palette. Add a simple center vein to the leaves, keeping the lines disconnected just a bit.

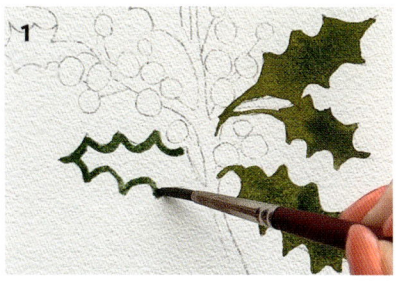
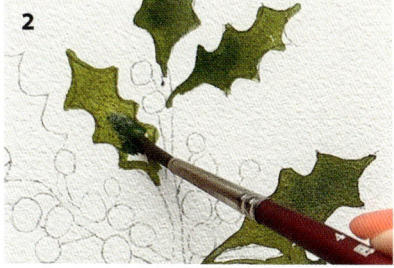
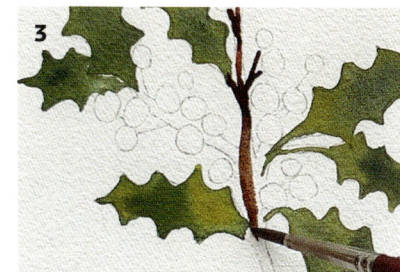
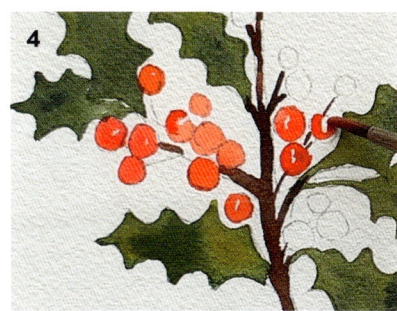
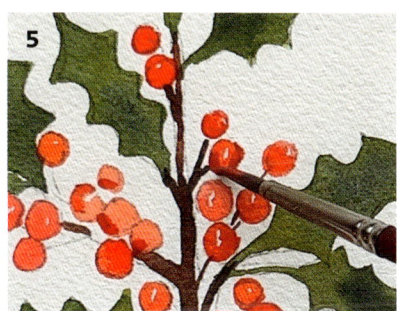
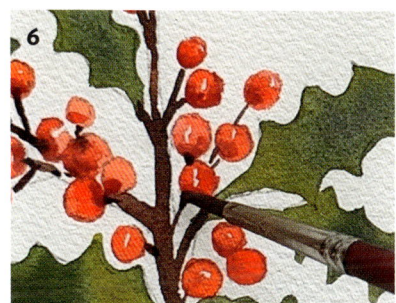
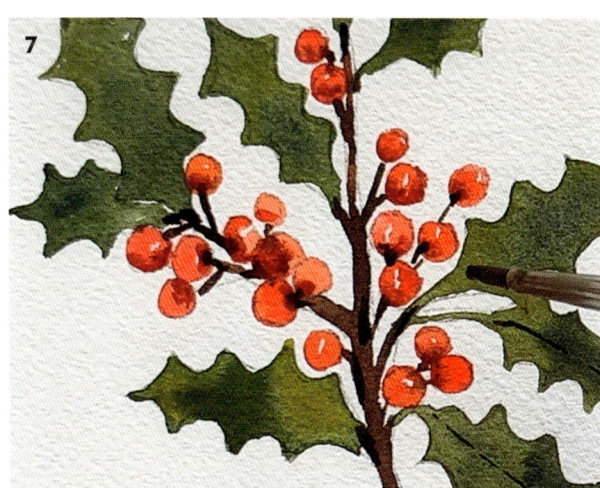
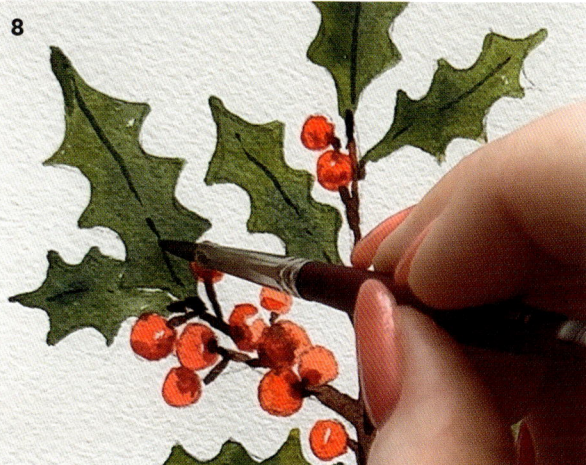

Quarto.com
WalterFoster.com

© 2026 Quarto Publishing
Text, Photos, Illustrations © 2026 Kristin Van Leuven

First Published in 2026 by Walter Foster Publishing, an imprint of
The Quarto Group, 100 Cummings Center, Suite 265-D,
Beverly, MA 01915, USA. T (978) 282-9590 F (978) 283-2742

EEA Representation, WTS Tax d.o.o., Žanova ulica 3,
4000 Kranj, Slovenia.
www.wts-tax.si

Walter Foster Publishing titles are also available at discount for
retail, wholesale, promotional, and bulk purchase. For details, contact
the Special Sales Manager by email at specialsales@quarto.com
or by mail at The Quarto Group, Attn: Special Sales Manager,
100 Cummings Center, Suite 265-D, Beverly, MA 01915, USA.

30 29 28 27 26   2 3 4 5

ISBN: 978-1-57715-696-3

Digital edition published in 2026
eISBN: 978-1-57715-697-0

Design and page layout: Kelley Galbreath

Printed in Guangdong, China TT022026